BEING HUMAN

BEING HUMAN

Bodies, Minds, Persons

ROWAN WILLIAMS

William B. Eerdmans Publishing Company
Grand Rapids, Michigan

Wm. B. Eerdmans Publishing Co.
4035 Park East Court SE, Grand Rapids, Michigan 49546
www.eerdmans.com

First published 2018 in Great Britain by
Society for Promoting Christian Knowledge, London, UK
Eerdmans edition published 2018
Printed in the United States of America

27 26 25 24 23 22 21 20 19 18   1 2 3 4 5 6 7 8 9 10

ISBN 978-0-8028-7656-0

Contents

Introduction

This book completes a sort of unintended trilogy, following earlier books, *Being Christian* and *Being Disciples*. It is less about the basics of Christian belief and behaviour and more about the sort of questions in our culture that make us wonder what 'real' humanity is like and whether our most central ideas about what is human are under threat in this environment. As these chapters suggest, there are grounds for being a bit concerned about our current models of human life and human well-being. No need to panic; but if we are to think and act in a way that helps to make the world more rather than less human – and humane – we do need more clarity than our culture usually gives us as to what we think is 'more' human. So the chapters of this book examine some sources of contemporary confusion, and outline some of the characteristics that we might look for in human lives when they are in touch with or in alignment with the grace and joy of what is ultimately true – with God and with the will of God, as Christians would say.

These pieces are a bit more demanding in some ways than most of the shorter talks collected in the earlier books, so it may help to give a quick sketch of each chapter to draw out the main arguments.

Chapter 1 looks at the question of what we understand by being conscious and self-conscious. A lot of popular scientific literature these days encourages us to think of the mind as a machine or the brain as a computer or whatever. But it's impossible to think consistently about being conscious without reference to our locality in a material world, without a sense of narrative, the story of a self, and without factoring in our relationships and our language.

So what is a 'person' in the light of all this? *Chapter 2* tries to suggest some answers. A person is not simply another object, and not something whose presence or absence we can decide just by applying a set of objective criteria. Persons are more than 'individuals'; they are both spiritual and material, and their uniqueness is fulfilled in community not in isolation and total independence.

And if we ask what it means to say that a person is both spiritual and material, we are in the territory covered by *Chapter 3*, which looks at body–mind relations in the light of some of the recent scientific discussions of left-brain and right-brain functions and the complex role of the body in what we call thinking. We think with our bodies because we have to learn how to find our way in a world of bodies. And this should make us wary of any picture of our humanity that isolates it or imagines our human knowing as being like beams from a lighthouse playing over a world of passive stuff – rather than being a process of rich interweaving of stimulus and imagining, worked out in and through bodies.

We are very much in love these days with the ideal of 'autonomy', self-direction, the independent control of our environment. *Chapter 4* looks at the ways in which religious faith helps us understand how we can be dependent without humiliation, as it also helps us deal with the educating of our instincts and passions, with the passing of time and the acceptance of our mortality. Part of the good news that faith offers is the realization that learning to depend on God and to live with (not in opposition to) our limits in time and the body is something that increases our freedom rather than reducing it.

And this means that in our life and our prayer we do not have to be afraid of letting go of the need to be in charge, to be explaining and organizing all the time. As Chapter 5 suggests, human beings who have grown into their full freedom will be at home with silence and openness before God. Which is also why good worship is worship that takes us beyond the urge to explain and manage, and leads us to take the time we need to open up to the endless richness of divine life that has been offered to us through the life and death and resurrection of Jesus.

In fact, we are brought back to the basics of belief again – to the conviction that to understand properly what our humanity really is we need to look to Jesus. The book ends with a sermon about the Ascension of Jesus as a sign that all the diverse aspects of human experience, including its darkest moments, are capable of being taken up and transfigured in the action of Jesus Christ.

Unless we have a coherent model of what sort of humanity we want to nurture in our society, we shall continue to be at sea over how we teach, how we vote, how we save and buy and sell, how we entertain ourselves, how we think about the beginning and the end of life. This little book will not provide once-and-for-all answers to the various questions this involves, but I hope it may help clarify what sort of priorities a Christian might want to have in mind in engaging with them; just a little bit of a manual of resistance to the forces – political, economic, psychological – that pressure us to be less than God wants us to be.

Once again, my thanks go to Philip Law and all at SPCK for their encouragement to pull together this group of talks and reflections, and their dedicated help in producing a publishable text.

1

What is consciousness?

The study of human consciousness encompasses an exceptionally wide range of questions in neuroscience and philosophy, as well as some questions that impact very directly on many of the things that theologians or ethicists most want to talk about. So although I won't be talking very much in this chapter about theology as such, I hope that some of the trails I lay might suggest some of the theological possibilities that arise in thinking through the fundamental questions about the nature of consciousness and what it is to be human.

But before embarking on the detailed questions, there is a general point worth remembering. 'The question of consciousness' is now a question that is best and most effectively addressed on the frontiers of different disciplines, so that the sort of book that has this kind of title will very often draw from physics, neuroscience in particular, philosophy, psychology, literature and many other fields. It's a helpful reminder that some of the rigid divisions of subject matter that so often afflict the academy won't quite do when fundamental issues of this sort are at stake. This has both positive and negative effects: positive, because conversations between different academic areas are among the most fertile discussions that happen in universities; negative, because the literature that can come out of this may be lacking in the rigour that applies in any one of those areas left to themselves. Some of what I say here will, I hope, help to identify those areas where lack of rigour is a problem, and doubtless a great deal more will illustrate the problem of lack of rigour in other ways. But I think it is worth beginning by reminding ourselves of this very significant fact in the current intellectual climate. While we talk, and talk freely, about ours being a very specialized era where people go more narrowly and deeply into questions than once they did, it is perhaps also the case that the biggest issues that confront us as a human race are issues that require a certain amount of multidisciplinary skill if we're to tackle them effectively.

The biggest issues that confront us as a human race are issues that require a certain amount of multidisciplinary skill if we're to tackle them effectively

Is the mind a machine?

Let me begin with two negative points about recent discussions of consciousness in some of the literature. There is a consensus in many quarters, philosophical and sci-

entific, that one thing we can confidently say about consciousness or the mind is that it is a kind of machine.
A recent book on the problem of consciousness by
Stanislas Dehaene concludes by saying, 'There is really
no problem in describing human beings as machines
with free will.'[1] I'll give some reasons for thinking there
are problems in a moment, but let me dwell for now on
why this metaphor of the machine is interesting.
Consciousness is mechanical, the brain is a kind of
machine, the brain is a kind of computer, we frequent-
ly hear. Therefore what we most need to know about
consciousness is what this machine's operations are. The
other frequent 'consensus' perspective that is offered by
philosophers and scientists follows from this: if consciousness is machine-like in important or definitive
ways, then of course it is a mistake to think that consciousness is, of its nature, something that registers what
is the case. At its most extreme, this leads some writers
to say that the idea of consciousness is itself a mistake.
Others have said, less radically, that there are no thoughts
that are thoughts *of* anything. A 'thought' is an operation
within the machine's workings.

To start off, I want to try and clear away the confusion
that seems to me inherent in both of those ways of thinking about the question, beginning with the metaphor of
the machine. The problem with thinking of consciousness

as machine-like, or the brain as a computer, is that this is precisely a *metaphor*, and a metaphor with a set of particularly complicated associations. A machine exits in order to solve problems; problems that are *extraneous to itself*. We design mechanical processes in order to produce specified functions. A machine fails if it does not deliver the function we have specified for it, so that an internal combustion engine which fails to drive a car but which very satisfactorily boils eggs is not a good machine. But in what sense can we say that consciousness in general, or the brain in particular, is a 'machine' in that sense? Is it something that exists in order to solve problems extraneous to itself? Prima facie the answer has to be no. At the very least, at the most reductive, the brain is an *organism*; and an organism is not exactly a machine. Organisms solve their own problems: in evolutionary history, organisms develop in order to deal with their own crises of adjusting to the environment. They are not there in order to solve problems outside themselves but modify what they are as well as what they do so as to maintain successful interaction with a diverse set of conditions.

As soon as the language of the machine comes into play, we have a major conceptual or definitional problem; and as soon as such language occurs in this discussion, it needs at once to be flagged with all kinds of warning signs. It is also interesting (and I'll come back to this a bit later) that the machine model tends to assume that the fundamental form of causality in the world is mechanical. The most important, the most basic, cause of relations is mechanical, entirely matters of input and output, not even exactly of stimulus and response. And that elides the many difficulties that still lie around the very notion of causality, in science and elsewhere. It carries with it a set of assumptions too about materiality, which once again I'll return to later; and it rather ignores the extremely complicated questions of how information and the exchange of information, both in natural and constructed systems, works causally. It ignores the issues of the 'emergent' properties of more and more complex systems, and it ignores the perspective offered by what is usually referred to as holism, that something may be more than the sum of its parts and have properties as a whole which do not correspond to the properties of any of its component parts.

Is the mind a mistake?

The machine model is one that we ought immediately to question. And of course if we do so question it there is less incentive to think that the language of consciousness might be a mistake, or that we might have to conclude that thoughts are thoughts about nothing in particular. But as soon as we've articulated this question in terms of a possible *mistake*, we see that there are intrinsic problems with it. Being mistaken is something that happens to, or in, consciousnesses. Internal combustion engines don't make mistakes. Machines do not make mistakes: they malfunction. But the notion of a mistake is that of a perception, a categorization of the world, being a bad fit with what is the case; and this is something we associate with consciousness itself. If you're at all interested in how to represent propositions logically, it's not possible to represent coherently the idea that consciousness is a mistake. If you define consciousness, as we are bound to, as precisely the sort of thing that makes mistakes, there's an infinite logical regress. The same applies to 'thoughts of nothing'. If I say my thoughts are thoughts about nothing, of course I am articulating a thought, which is about thoughts. And again I cannot get out of that particular loop; even within our thinking about thinking, we can make a distinction between thinking of different sorts of nothing – bear with me. I can *say* I am thinking of a square circle, but I am there quite literally thinking of no thing – there is nothing that can conceivably correspond to that, there is no coherent logical way of representing that thought. I could say I am thinking of a unicorn: I can think of a picture of a creature that doesn't exist. I am thinking about nothing that is instantiated in the world, but something that has a symbolic or legendary identity. Or I could think about things that are really there. I could think not about unicorns but about zebras, and then I'm thinking of something. The point of this rather laboured excursion is simply that our thoughts are, as thoughts, 'intentional'. The concept of a thought is the concept of something that is *about* something. Once again we are back to the question of definition. If consciousness is a mistake, I am already importing consciousness into the word 'mistake'. If thought is of nothing but itself, I am exporting from thought the assumption we always make about our thinking – that it is about something, even if it is sometimes about something that has no actual instances.

My point in starting with these two negative categorizations is simply to put down some very clear markers about the easy mistakes that are sometimes made by those who don't approach this question with enough philosophical rigour. 'Consciousness is a machine' and 'consciousness is a mistake' may both have a certain glamour, a certain seductive simplicity about them as statements. Neither of them can be made to make sense. So, whatever we say at the end of the day about the relationship between consciousness and the material world, between the self and the brain, we cannot reduce it to either of those propositions.

But if those two negatives are set aside, if the reduction-ist consensus is rejected, what then are the positives we might suggest? In the next part of what I want to say, I'd like to draw attention to four aspects of our language and thinking about consciousness that might go a little further towards answering the rashly ambitious question that forms the title of this chapter.

Consciousness is located

First of all, when we speak of human consciousness, we speak of something that is *located* somewhere. My con-sciousness is *this* point of view. It is what's characterized by the first per-son singular. It is a strategy by which this material identity here charts a path through a material environ-ment. It has sometimes been said

> When we speak of human consciousness, we speak of something that is located *somewhere*

that human knowledge begins in the experience of bump-ing into things: quite literally, as a child, one finds one's way around things, so that one stops bumping into them sooner or later. But of course it is not just about the mater-ial self charting a path through material objects. I men-tioned a moment ago the ways in which information works in our world. The world of cause and interaction in which we live is not, with due respect to seventeenth-century and indeed sometimes twenty-first-century models, a

8

world in which small solid objects bump against each other, as if the world is a very large snooker table. Change happens and interaction happens because information is exchanged. And information may be exchanged at very simple, basic molecular levels, and it may also be exchanged in slightly less materially confined ways by words being spoken or read, associations being awoken in those hearing or reading, and fresh configurations of language appearing. My location as a consciousness is not just my ability to map a world of things and stuff around me; it's also my capacity to map a world of communication; to place myself within a network of interchanging information from the molecular level to the level of speech and the concept. I live in a world where I don't simply bump into things, but a world where I bump into *signs* – that is, things that *communicate*, that trigger further symbolic communication, that produce further utterance and make a difference at that level. Consciousness is located: within the material world and within the world of language, about which more later.

To try and think through what we mean habitually and non-technically by 'consciousness', without registering that fundamental reality of a location – what one philosopher called a 'zero point of orientation'[2] – is to misunderstand the nature of the question. But if consciousness is located, localized, to this point of orientation, it's a matter of charting lines of relation with other material agents, realities, processes and symbolic processes; and then the notion of *relatedness* becomes equally key to the idea of consciousness. So the second positive point I want to make about consciousness has to do with *relationality*, the way in which having a point of view here, my 'zero point of orientation', takes for granted that there are other points of orientation. To be immediately aware of being *here* is also to be aware of others being *there*.

Consciousness is relational

To take this a bit further: if my presence here is a matter of my decoding the signs that are given to me materially and in other ways around me, then decoding those signs, registering and organizing the information I receive, requires me to do some imagining – to imagine another point of view. My consciousness is not simply registering a lot of impressions that are coming to me from a mechanical world generating impressions outside; I don't simply register stimuli and receive passively: I engage in a kind of systematized guesswork. I put myself in the position of another. I understand that while I can't see the back of my head, you can. I understand that while I am speaking, you may be imagining many things, and raising all kinds of interesting questions in your mind about when this chapter is going to finish, or when it's going to begin to make sense, or whatever. I as author imagine my readers. I imagine what makes sense; but much more than that, much more basically than that, to have a sense of any object (including my own body) is to presuppose a number of points of view. I construct a 'synoptic', a 'walking around' picture, of an object, a person, something that I encounter, by imagining other points of view. But I can't even imagine my own body as a unit without imagining another point of view. To think of myself as a body, to be conscious of myself as a body, is to be conscious of other people's consciousness.

> *To think of myself as a body, to be conscious of myself as a body, is to be conscious of other people's consciousness*

That's my second positive point. Consciousness as we normally think about it has a relational dimension. I can't think without thinking of the other. I can't even think of my body, this zero point of orientation, without understanding that it's an object to another. *I am seen*, I am heard, I am understood; and whether I am talking about myself in a general and vague sense, or talking about my body as a specific organic unit, I am bound to be imagining what is not exhausted by one solitary viewpoint. To have a point of view is to understand that the world is constructed out of diverse points of orientation.

11

And this means that my consciousness is mobile, engaged, incomplete: because I can't construct the idea of any object without supposing a diversity of points of view, I know that my point of view is always partial, and to be conscious of myself is to be aware of myself as a node point in a web of information exchange, which corporately constructs the idea of objects, selves, persons. To be conscious is, primitively, to be able to find my way around a material environment without bumping into things. It is the ability to calculate distance and speed – as, for example, when another physical object, like a human body, is coming towards me (am I going to bump into that person?). But it's also about how I 'read' a face: what are the signs that are being given by the person that I am speaking to or listening to? It's about being able to argue to a wider context than that which is simply defined by what is registered primitively as stimuli for my senses now.

Consciousness is co-operative, and it's in this light that we might reflect on some of the remarkable work of writers such as Iain McGilchrist, a neuroscientist with a significant philosophical and literary education, who notes that, because of the bicameral nature of the brain (the fact that it consists of two hemispheres), there are different kinds of awareness operative in us – one cluster of operations dealing with detail, small-scale recognition, the other dealing with constructive and connecting perception.[3] And while that's a very crude breakdown of how the hemispheres of the brain work (these operations don't belong exclusively to one hemisphere or the other), it's not completely misleading in that it reminds us that our habitual unexamined consciousness works in widely diverse ways. We see how that works, to some extent, when we see what happens in the case of brain malfunction, so that the situation of someone (and there are such cases) who can recognize noses, eyes, mouths but not faces, becomes a kind of key to understanding how our consciousness, collaboratively, within its own organic terms, puts together complex objects *as* objects. There is always a range of operations in the brain making the connections that allow larger pictures to be seen, allowing us to know, by imagining, not simply by registering.

Interestingly, one of the most significant contributions to this subject was made about a hundred years ago by a young German Jewish philosopher, Edith Stein, a pupil of the great philosopher Edmund Husserl, who edited some of his manuscripts for publication. She published in 1916 a doctoral dissertation on the problem of *empathy*, in which she argued with great sophistication that consciousness itself was collaborative, empathetic – in the sense that to be conscious of anything, one had to have the capacity to imagine another point of view (it was she who used the phrase I borrowed earlier about the 'zero point of orientation'). It anticipates by several decades some of the work done after the Second World War in France by another great philosopher, Maurice Merleau-Ponty. (Edith Stein's work is also significant for some of us not least because, to the great surprise of many, she converted to Catholicism, became a Carmelite nun and died in Auschwitz, where what she had written about consciousness and identity was rather more than just a set of academic challenges.)

Consciousness is a continuous narrative

If consciousness is local, about different points of view, it is also intrinsically about several interlocking or intersecting points of view. It is collaborative, it is social, simply in the sense that to imagine anything, person or object, including my own body, I need to imagine another person seeing. And this leads on to a third positive category for consciousness. My point of view, my first-person perspective, is something that is always constructed, articulated and explored, partly in terms of where it's come *from*. I assume continuity; I assume there's an identity between the perceptions and interactions of which I have been part in the past and what is now going on. Constant shifts of physical movement and the lapse of time don't dissolve the notion that the point of view I inhabit, the first person that I articulate, is a consistent, a continuous reality. And despite assaults from both philosophy and bits of the neuroscientific world, it's extremely difficult to know how we would begin to talk about consciousness without that sense of continuity and time; so that the third positive category we might apply to consciousness is *narrative.*

Consciousness is located, it's relational and it's a narrative, something fixed with reference to past situations as well as current stimuli. It's involved, at the most basic level, with the recognition of stimuli in connection with previous stimuli. It's also, of course, confusingly and often disturbingly tied in with memory, images of the past, whose function we can't easily determine. My capacity to remember what I don't need to remember, and indeed what I don't want to remember at times, is one of the burdens of consciousness about which people write so much. I recall a poignant moment when a very senior academic of my acquaintance, many years ago, spoke of the 'curse' of near total recall, an over-developed memory, an inability to forget or marginalize painful and difficult recollections. It's another of those things that's not captured at all well by the machine model of consciousness. We don't know, and we can't know at any given moment, exactly what function is served by the bits of memory that come in and out of awareness, but our consciousness draws in those floating impressions from the past, works on the assumption that they are part of a single story, and very often works overtime to synthesize or make sense of those floating impressions. There is an intrinsic significance in our understanding of consciousness of the history of doing and being done to. The his-

The stories others tell about me are not necessarily the stories I would tell about myself

tory of what we've done and what has been done to us, shaping awareness now, is something that we must register as a central part of what it is to be conscious; and this also gives us a new perspective on the relationality that I mentioned earlier. Not only do I narrate – tell a story about myself – I am also aware that I'm somebody about whom stories are told. *Others* see me as a continuum, as I see myself, and, as any conversation at any depth will reveal, the stories others tell about me are not necessarily the stories I would tell about myself. (Anybody who's spent any time in public life will of course feel this rather acutely.) I am a narrator but I am also 'narrated'. I am agent, but I am acted upon. I see and I am seen. And to be conscious is therefore to be aware not simply of being a subject – a first-person agent – but also of being an object: someone spoken about, someone of whom stories are told.

Consciousness is a shared language

So, fourth, and finally among these positive characterizations of consciousness: consciousness is always bound up with *language*. That's not to say that I have no thoughts that I don't express in words. It's not to say that my consciousness is a complete verbal catalogue of the things that happen to me in my mind (which is a whole bundle of philosophical misunderstandings). Consciousness is not the deliberate registering of the 'contents of the mind', but it is bound in with the capacity to respond to and to develop or complicate the basic information exchanges that are going on in me at every level. Or to put it in plain English, speaking changes things. To say something introduces new possibilities. To be conscious, to be part of this narrative, relational, localized life, which I've described as the life of consciousness, is to be a speaker – somebody generating signs and symbols; an agent inviting listening, interpretation, and so on. Speaking changes things – and, to put it at its most provocative, a theory of evolution potentially changes how evolution works. When we have a theory about how something in the world around us works, we have implicitly a capacity to make a difference to that working. So our language, our generation of symbols, our invitation to interpretation and exchange, is, it seems, intrinsic to this picture of consciousness as embedded in relation, locality and storytelling. It's because of all these things that the malfunctions or disorders of consciousness are so painful to us. Those whose spatial sense is distorted; those whose awareness of relationality is limited; those whose memory has been affected by developments within their brain; those who lose symbol-generating capacity or never have it – all of such human beings we recognize *as* persons, and as persons wrestling with exceptional challenges. We don't write them off as persons, but nor do we think they're simply an ordinary variation of the type, which is why, in thinking through issues around consciousness, I find some of the most suggestive, creative and challenging insights come from looking at how people work with those living with autistic conditions, for example, or with varying kinds of dementia. It's when we see malfunction or challenge of this nature that we begin to see also what we take for granted. In doing so, as I say, we don't write off another as *lacking* consciousness; we are prompted to ask some basic questions about what we mean by consciousness, and what precisely it is that has varied from our expectations.

Before moving on to my final section, let me just recap once more. Negatively speaking, I've attempted to put on one side the popular but deeply fallacious models that regard consciousness as machinery or mistake. I have argued that in our habitual reflection on how consciousness works we ordinarily assume, pretty much without argument, a number of aspects without which we couldn't begin to make sense of how the world works – locality, relationality, narrative, language. And it's surprising and sometimes rather dismaying that some quite technical conversations about the nature of consciousness, whether scientific or philosophical, in the last decade or two, have been rather reluctant to engage with some of these features, and with the issue of language in particular.

Resisting reductionism

In this final section, I want to do two things. One is simply to ask the question of where the reductive passion comes from. And the second, unsurprisingly, is to trail a few theological thoughts before you, to see where this might go as we take it into another area.

But first of all, why the reductive passion? Why the concern to insist on mechanism and mistake? The philosopher and physician Raymond Tallis, in his book *Reflections of a Metaphysical Flâneur*, offers some very apposite insight on this.[4] One essay, which has the unforgettable title, 'You chemical scum, you', begins with the words, 'I am sick of being insulted. There seems to be a competition among some contemporary thinkers to dream up the most hostile descriptions of homo sapiens, a species of which I am proud to be an example.' And he quotes from a number of distinguished scientists, including the great Stephen Hawking, who have come out with excitingly and strikingly reductive accounts of humanity. In the 1990s, Stephen Hawking said, 'The human race is just a chemical scum on an average-sized planet, orbiting round a very average-sized star, in the outer suburb of one of a million galaxies' (hence the title 'You chemical scum, you').[5] Tallis raises and begins to answer the question of why it is there seems to be such a passion to reduce what we can say about a conscious mind, let alone the freedom of the will. In the light of his discussion, I think there are at least three things going on here.

The first is something I touched on very briefly earlier, and that is a simple philosophical crudity about causality, materiality and matters like that. We are tempted constantly to look for *the* basic structure, that to which everything can be reduced. All of biology is really chemistry, all of chemistry is really physics, all of physics is really mathematics, all of mathematics – that's when things get a bit complicated. But, the point is that the reductive concern – extremely important for certain practical purposes – can become a search for the least adorned, the most fundamental pattern or structure we can come up with, while ignoring the fact that this, in Tallis's words, 'makes all appearances disappear. Nothing is really a thing.' When we have said that everything can be reduced to this or that equation, we have actually said nothing of any great substance; we have simply said there is a mathematical process without which this would not be what it is. But given what has already been said about the emergent properties of complex systems, the fact that there are wholes whose capacities and properties are more than any of their parts, reductionism as a systematic, global principle is simply intellectually incoherent. That there are more organized, more complex ways of describing a set of physical phenomena is not a matter of scum on the water. It is a matter of recognizing that with any situation, any set of circumstances in the material world, there will be a variety of proper descriptions depending on where you are sitting.

> *Reductionism as a systematic, global principle is simply intellectually incoherent*

It is perfectly true that a performance of Bach's solo cello suites is a set of physical operations. Catgut and string co-operate in producing certain vibrations. The usefulness of that as a description of what's going on, the usefulness of it, for example, in adjudicating between the different interpretations of Paul Tortelier and Yo-Yo Ma of the Bach Cello Suites is nil. And we need to recall that what seems to be a compelling reductive version is telling you nothing, except that this is an intrinsic element in a complex reality. Behind that reductionism, as again I've suggested, is what's often an unexamined notion of matter. Daniel Dennett (a philosopher for whom I have a great deal of respect) has said that we have to bear in mind in any discussion of consciousness that there is only one kind of *stuff*.[6] And while that's very tempting, I want to know a little bit more about what he means by 'stuff'. Because, of course, the world is not full of stuff; the world is a very complex set of inter-actions of information-bearing energy. And when you've said that, and recognized that the word 'information' is, as the professionals say, 'analogical' (that is, that it works on a number of different levels in interestingly different ways), it's no longer particularly interesting to say 'there's one sort of stuff'. The world we inhabit is not a world where little solid things bump into each other and nudge each other around. It is a world in which information and instructions (interesting we use these nakedly intel-lectual metaphors) are conveyed through material exchanges of energy, and the more we analyse those material exchanges of energy, the less it looks like little bits of stuff. So my first guess at a diagnosis of why this sort of reductionism is popular would simply be that there is a real lack of philosophical precision and even consistency within the language being used.

My second suggested diagnosis is a little more hostile. Ludwig Wittgenstein said in the 1930s, 'It is *charming* to destroy prejudice.'[7] That is to say that if somebody tells you that x is 'only' really y, that's very attractive. If somebody can tell you that you need not bother about a certain aspect of reality because what is *really* going on is this, you have made a very powerful, compelling and seductive statement. You have admitted somebody to an inner circle of those who know What Is Really Going On; and we all know how immensely appealing that is. To be told that we are nothing but chemical scum gives us, paradoxically, the thrill of being insiders. We are the chemical scum who *know* we are chemical scum: that is a powerful, appealing, cool position to be in. Power is an issue here, and it's another one of those aspects of this whole question which, I believe, is insufficiently discussed. To speculate about consciousness as mechanical or mistaken, to say there is no such thing as a point of view, may be an agreeable fantasy within the pages of a scientific textbook. It is rather different when applied to the reality of an actual other person and his or her point of view. It is rather difficult to deduce from it any kind of justifiable ethical seriousness about human diversity. I said a moment ago that reductionism is a permission to ignore certain levels or aspects of what we in fact perceive, and I would say that any intellectual strategy that gives you permission to ignore some level of legitimate description is morally deeply dangerous, as well as being philosophically odd. But the charm remains: the admission to the inner circle, those who really know.

My third and final point leads on to some concluding unscientific and vaguely theological reflections. Much more speculatively, I suspect that the animus of certain kinds of scientist and philosopher towards the models of consciousness and indeed of freedom, or of personal identity, that I have been working with reflects a faint residual feeling that there is something about consciousness that intrinsically leaves the question of the sacred on the table. Consciousness as local yet also relational, as receptive and also creative, as narrative, as having to do with speaking and being spoken about, seeing and being seen, as the generation of symbol, is something that sits, if not comfortably, at least coherently, with that model of the universe that religious people on the whole take for granted, a model of the universe in which intelligibility and intelligence are omnipresent: in which there is no such thing as 'dead matter'; in which there is always a speaking, an invitation, a summons to engage, which for the theologian is bound up with the nature of creation itself, with the idea that all that we are, as a finite set of systems in the universe, is as it is because it responds to a fundamental communication of intelligence or information – or indeed 'communion'. Receptivity and co-operation, a sense of limit or incompleteness, symbol and the transparency of symbols – all of these have their natural location in the kind of human discourse that takes for granted what may be called 'the sacred' in general, but that I am much happier in calling God, within the context of a doctrine of creation, as making sense against the background of a God whose will or purpose or character it is to share what his life is.

To elaborate this further would of course lead us straight into considerations of doctrine, which are not the primary purpose of this chapter. But I hope that in what I have said so far about this vastly complicated and enticing and frustrating borderland, where physics and philosophy and psychology blend, what I have said so far about this may just make some sense of what many thinkers have wanted to say in the last century or more, which is that a loss of the sense of the sacred, a loss of the sense of being answerable to an intelligible gift, from beyond ourselves, in the long run entails more than simply the loss of God; it may entail the loss of the distinctively human. And if there is one great intellectual challenge for our day, it is the pervasive sense that we are in danger of losing our sense of the human.

If there is one great intellectual challenge for our day, it is the pervasive sense that we are in danger of losing our sense of the human

Whether or not any of my readers would agree that to recover a sense of the human you have to turn to theology, I won't take for granted. I note that there are impressive and sophisticated critics of reductionism – including Raymond Tallis and John Gray, whose book *The Soul of the Marionette*[8] raises some of these questions – who do not move from an argument against reductionism to any sympathy for theism. But the questions are undoubtedly on the table: the loss of the human, the philosophy that some people describe as 'transhuman', the notion that we can become more than human, that our organic identity can be superseded by various kinds of cyber technology – all of this ought to make us anxious about where exactly we look in anchoring our sense of the distinctly human; anchoring confidence in our own consciousness. While I don't delude myself for a moment that I have answered the question posed in the title of this chapter, I hope that these remarks may have illustrated why it's a question that matters immensely to us as a culture, and why some of the popular and apparently simple responses to the question won't do, logically, psychologically or even scientifically.

For reflection or discussion

1 Who are the most significant people in your life at present, and how do you imagine they see you in relation to them?

2 Can you identify some key moments or episodes in your
life story that have shaped your consciousness of yourself and the way you view the world around you?

2

What is a person?

In 1955 a Russian theologian living in Paris published a short essay on 'The Theological Notion of the Human Person'. It was quite a technical study, which focused largely on the vocabulary of the early Christians, but it is in fact something of a watershed in modern theological thinking. From that relatively brief discussion in 1955 a whole strand of thinking within the Eastern Christian world developed, and has in turn affected the Western Christian world. It united its emphases and concerns with some very deep themes that were already being explored in Western Christianity earlier in the twentieth century. But by the end of the 1960s, it was possible to trace what many people have called a 'personalist' style of theology emerging across the Christian world in its diverse traditions – a style of theology deeply connected with a particular way of analysing relations.

The theologian in question was Vladimir Lossky. Exiled from Russia at the beginning of the 1920s, he died prematurely in the 1950s, having produced a rather small body of work – but a body of work that is of significance out of all proportion to its size. In this particular essay the substantive conclusion that he proposes is this: as Christians, he said, we don't yet have a proper vocabulary for distinguishing between two things that it's absolutely vital to hold apart. Those two things are, first, something that is simply *one unique instance of its kind* and, on the other hand, that *quality*, whatever it is, that makes a conscious thing of this kind '*irreducible to its nature*'. Let's pause on this to begin with.

Something that is simply 'one unique instance of its kind' is an object that stands alongside other objects, distinguished by certain particular features. There are a lot of dogs, they all share the characteristic of being dogs, only one of them is Fido, one of them is Rover, and so on. That in itself simply tells you there are lots of examples of this kind of thing. But it doesn't quite do duty when it comes to thinking about what we are like as persons.

What makes us persons?

There is something about us as conscious agents that doesn't simply boil down to being one example of a kind of thing. That's not to say you have to search for some specific *element* that makes us personal rather than otherwise – intelligence or freedom or whatever. It's more like an observation that when we talk about being 'a person', we're talking of something about us as a whole that isn't specified, that isn't defined, just by listing facts that happen to be true about us. Lossky says that there isn't really a concept that will do this work at all. We simply haven't got the word. We know what we mean when we distinguish between personal and impersonal, and we know roughly what we mean when we talk about persons in relation. But we struggle to pin this down, this idea that somehow we are not to be reduced to our nature, to the things that happen to be true about us. And Lossky says that just as when we try to talk about God, we're left here with a kind of space, a kind of mystery, something we can't really manage in third-person descriptive terms. Here's what he says towards the end of his essay:

> Under these conditions, it will be impossible for us to form a concept of the human person, and we will have to content ourselves with saying: 'person' signifies the irreducibility of man to his nature – 'irreducibility' and not 'something irreducible' or 'something which makes man irreducible to his nature' precisely because it cannot be a question here of 'something' distinct from 'another nature' but of someone who is distinct from his own nature, of someone who goes beyond his nature while still containing it, who makes it exist as human nature by this overstepping of it.[1]

30

Third-person categories, description at arm's length, don't work. Something more needs to be said. We establish ourselves as human by stepping beyond the bundle of facts that we might use to define humanity in general, even the bundle of facts that distinguish us from another example of the same kind of thing, that might distinguish Fido from Rover. What makes me a person, and what makes me *this* person rather than another, is not simply a set of facts. Or rather it's the enormous fact of my being here rather than elsewhere, being in these relations with those around me, being a child of these parents, a parent of these children, the friend of x, the not-so-intimate friend of y. I stand in the middle of a network of relations, the point where the lines cross. While it may be true to say I am the sum total of all the things that have happened to me, as soon as I *say* I am the sum total of all the things that have happened to me, I change the sum total of the things that are true about me. I make a difference to the facts of nature. I do so because of, and in the light of, the relations I'm involved in. And by saying and acting and responding, I create fresh facts. But there in the middle is that elusive, mysterious area, that something which is not just a something, not

What makes me a person, and what makes me this *person rather than another, is not simply a set of facts*

31

just a capacity, not just a fact about me, something mysterious, something not open to third-person analysis.

So as a person I embody, I carry with me, all the things that have happened to me – the things that are, as a matter of fact, true about me. But moment by moment I respond to that agenda in different ways, I activate what is there in different ways, and I set up new chains of connection and relationship. A person, in other words, is the point at which relationships intersect, where a difference may be made and new relations created. It's in virtue of this that Christians are able to look at any and every human individual and say that the same kind of mystery is true of all of them, and that therefore the same kind of reverence or attention is due to all of them. We can never say, for example, that such and such a person has the full set of required characteristics for being a human person and therefore deserves our respect, and that such and such another individual doesn't have the full set and therefore doesn't deserve our respect.

This of course is why – historically and at the present day – Christians worry about those kinds of human beings who may not tick all the boxes but whom we still believe to be worthy of respect, whether it's those not yet born, those severely disabled, those dying, those in various ways marginal and forgotten. It's why Christians conclude that attention is due to all of them. What that means, in specific circumstances, we may still argue a lot about, but this is non-negotiably where we start from. The underlying point is quite simply that there is no way of, as it were, presenting a human individual with an examination paper and according him or her the reward of our attention or respect only if he or she gets above a certain percentage of marks. Any physical, organically real member of the human race deserves that respect, never mind how many boxes are ticked.

Another way of putting this is that we ascribe *personal* dignity or worth to people – to human individuals – because of the sense that, in relationship, each of us has a presence or a meaning in someone else's existence. We live in another's life. To be the point where lines of a relationship intersect means that we can't simply lift some

Each of us has a presence or a meaning in someone else's existence

abstract thing called 'the person' out of it all. We're talking about a reality in which people enter into the experience, the aspiration, the sense of self, of others. And that capacity to live in the life of another – to have a life in someone else's life – is part of the implication of this profound mysteriousness about personal reality. Deny this, and you are back with that deeply unsatisfactory model in which somebody decides who is going to count as human.

There was a phase in science fiction writing about 20 or 30 years ago where the question often came up of how you might recognize something as human on another planet or in some cyborg future. How might you accord to some other being the status of a person? How might you imagine conversing with that being? It's a good question to ask as a thought experiment, but as soon as you try to answer it in terms of what I've called 'ticking boxes' – they have this or that characteristic – you've rather missed the point. You would only really discover whether you could treat them as a person by a longish process of trying to form a relationship, trying to converse, trying to see what sort of exchange emerged as you related to that other. There are rules of thumb; there are helpful shortcuts we can apply. Very broadly speaking, 99 times out of 100, it's something to do with language that helps us decide how to treat, and whether to treat, someone else as a person. And language of course means not only the words we speak but gestures, the flicker of an eyelid, the movement of a hand. But even that doesn't quite do it. At the end of the day we can say this is something we could discover only by taking time and seeing if a relationship could be built.

Here is another theological philosopher, this time a Roman Catholic, writing about this subject – the German Catholic philosopher Robert Spaemann:

Each organism naturally develops a system that interacts with its environment. Each creature stands at the centre of its own world. The world only discloses itself as that which can do something for us, something becomes meaningful in light of the interest we take in it. To see the other as other, to see myself as thou over against him, to see myself as constituting an environment for other centres of being, thus stepping out from the centre of my world, is an eccentric position that opens up a realm beyond substance. We find in ourselves the idea of the absolute, the infinite, as that which cannot be derived, as Descartes noted, from our finite and conditioned nature.[2]

As human beings in relationship we sense that our environment is created by a relation with other persons, we create an environment for them, and in that exchange – that mutuality – we discover what 'person' means. That's at the heart of what I want to reflect on a bit further in this chapter, the distinction between that mysterious, relational, conversational, environment-building activity that we call 'the person' and the individual as simply one example of a certain kind of thing.

Individual or personal?

In modern debate we quite often find ourselves faced with the alternative of individualism or communitarianism, the individual or the community. I suggest that that's not quite the right polarity to start from. It's not the individual and the community, but the individual and the person that we need to begin with – the difference between two ways of imagining and understanding what we are as agents, as speakers, as presences in the world. We can build into our sense of ourselves the 'individual' feeling, that basically we're just the centre of a world or one example of a certain kind of thing. Or we can take the risk of the second kind of talk about ourselves, the personal – more frustrating, more elusive, and yet more adequate to what we actually as human beings do and say most of the time – but I'll come back to that later.

Behind all this lies one very basic theological assumption, which Lossky in his essay underlines and which goes back a very long way in Christian thought – at least as far

Before anything else happens I am in relation to a non-worldly, non-historical everlasting attention and love, which is God

as St Augustine at the beginning of the fifth century. This assumption is that, before anything or anyone is in relation with anything or anyone else, it's in relation to *God*. And, said Augustine, the deeper I go into the attempt to understand myself, who and what I am, the more I find that I am *already* grasped, addressed, engaged with. I can't dig deep enough in myself to find an abstract self that's completely divorced from relationship. So, for St Augustine and the Christian tradition, before anything else happens I am in relation to a non-worldly, non-historical everlasting attention and love, which is God.

But if that is true of us, if our first relationship is with that energy that made us and sustains us in being, then of course, when I look around, my neighbour is also always somebody who is already in a relation with God before they're in a relation with me. That means that there's a very serious limit on my freedom to make of my neighbour what I choose, because, to put it very bluntly, they don't belong to me, and their relation to me is not all that is true of them, or even the most important thing that is true of them. That's true of everything in the world in a certain sense – which is one reason why there's a good Christian ground for being concerned about the environment. But it's true in a very intense sense of other persons, who see me as I see them, who relate to me and affect me as I relate to and affect them. I'm not on my own and I can't pretend that the basic form of my relation with the world is this little atom here controlling and mapping and planning all those other little atoms out there. I'm seen, I'm engaged with, and before even human engagement and vision is that relationship with God at the root of everything.

This is one of the most fundamental differences between an individualist and a personalist perspective on our lives as particular people and our lives as a society. Human dignity, the unconditional requirement that we attend with reverence to one another, rests firmly on this conviction that the other is already related to something that isn't me. And without that conviction we are in serious ethical trouble. That's why some people like to say, as Spaemann does in the book I quoted earlier, that there is a connection between the notion of human dignity and the notion of the sacred – not only the specific ways in which this or that religion talks about the 'sacred', but in the sense that there is in the other something utterly demanding of reverence, something which I cannot simply master or own or treat as an object like other objects. For the Christian, and for most religious believers, this is firmly rooted in the notion that the other, the human other, is already *related* – in other words, outside my power and my control.

I think we can push this further and say that when we claim human dignity, when we claim the right to be respected – when we claim our 'human rights', in fact – we're not just asserting that somewhere in us there is something making imperative demands. We're trying to affirm a *place*, a proper place, in relation with others. We're trying to affirm that we are embedded in relationship. I am,

I am, and I have value, because I am seen by and engaged with love

and I have value, because I am seen by and engaged with love – ideally, the love we experience humanly and socially, but, beyond and behind this, always and unconditionally the love of God. And the service of others' rights or dignity is, in this perspective, simply the search to *echo* this permanent attitude of love, attention, respect, which the Creator gives to what is made.

A language about human rights that is simply about some fact in us that makes it imperative that other people respect us can become very dry and very abstract. A language of human rights that is about the search for proper, mutual attention and reverence for a universal dignity has a bit more energy and I think a bit more depth. But of course, as Spaemann indicates in his essay already quoted, to step outside the realm of the individual – the one thing of its kind, the centre of its universe – to step outside that, to respond actively and creatively to our environment, to shape and alter our environment, to *be* an environment for others and to *be* the environment they create, to go 'beyond our nature', all this requires acts of faith. Living *as a person* is a matter of faith – stepping out in all these ways.

It is in many ways a lot easier to believe and to act as though each was in fact an atom, a world to itself. It is somehow very typical of the modern sense of self that when we speak about 'self-confidence' these days, we're often talking about relying on something that is *in* us – rather than having the courage to engage, to venture out, to be confident enough to *exchange* perspectives, truths, insights, to move into a particular kind of conversation or dialogue. I turn here to another influential writer, not a theologian this time but a sociologist, Richard Sennett of the London School of Economics, whose book *Together* touches on some of these matters. Here he is speaking about this question and quoting from the Russian philosopher Mikhail Bakhtin: 'A conversation affirms man's faith in his own experience. For creative understanding it is immensely important for the person to be located outside the object of his or her understanding.'[3]

Instead of trying to absorb things into ourselves, or to be absorbed into things outside ourselves, we seek to engage. We seek to set up a relationship; and this is a venture of courage which requires self-confidence, not in the terms of being assured that there is something solid inside us, but to be assured that we are related already to something that holds us, engages us and carries us through. Without that we end up with what Sennett elsewhere speaks of in terms of alienation from others, an individualized withdrawal, which, he says, 'seems the perfect recipe for complacency. You take for granted people like yourself and simply don't care about those who aren't like you.

More, whatever their problems are, it's their problem. Individualism and indifference become twins.' And he quotes from the great nineteenth-century French writer Alexis de Tocqueville, who in his second volume of *Democracy in America*, published in 1840, wrote, 'Each person, withdrawn into himself behaves as though he is a stranger to the destiny of all the others.'[4]

And that, for de Tocqueville and for Sennett, is the opposite of a personalist approach. If we begin from an *individualist* perspective, if we assume we are each of us a world to ourselves, that there is in us some solid core that sustains who we are independent of anything else, we end up alienated from the destiny of others.

If we assume we are each of us a world to ourselves, we end up alienated from the destiny of others

If we begin from the assumption that we are standing always in the midst of a network of relations, we don't ever know whose destiny or whose reality will and won't affect ours. That's a risky place to be, and it may indeed seem simpler, as Sennett says, to withdraw.

But part of the force of Sennett's analysis is that he applies these rather abstract ideas to some features of our world today and suggests that we're seeing more and more the evolution of an 'uncooperative self' – a self that assumes that what comes first is this isolated interior core which then negotiates its way around relations with others but always has the liberty of hurrying back indoors. He says that if you look at how labour, production and business work across the centuries, you see a gradual trend towards this uncooperative self, away from a sense of belonging with each other and taking responsibility for each other. Part of the purpose of this book, and indeed of other writings by Sennett, is to ask exactly what has gone wrong and exactly how might we get around it or rethink it.

An aspect of this which, Sennett notes in passing and which other philosophers and writers have observed at greater length, is that if you do still take for granted a basic individualist model, the hard core to which everything has got to accommodate itself, you drift towards a steady expectation that the best relationship you can be in to the world is *control*. The best place to be is a place where you can never be surprised. We want to control what's strange, and we want to control what doesn't fall under our immediate power. We're uneasy with limits that we can't get beyond because limits, of whatever kind, remind us that there are some things that are just going to be strange and difficult wherever we are and however hard we work at them. This can show itself in our corporate unease with limits, our exploitation of the environment, our expectation of an endless spiral of prosperity.

It can manifest in individual ways and in the aspiration for the perfect body, the perfect marriage, the perfect home and the perfect job. Here is a modern psychotherapist, Patricia Gosling, writing about this in a recent book:

> One sees [this notion of perfection and perfectibility] in the current obsession with the perfect body, the perfect home, the perfect lifestyle. One sees it getting out of control in mounting personal debt, in anorexia nervosa, in that slogan of Gestalt Theory that 'we can become anything we want to be'. Not true; and in that denial of reality lies a denial of our biological roots. Yes, we all have undeveloped potential. However it is also true that we each have our limitations, innate and circumstantial. The skill of living a satisfying life lies in using the transitional space between the two.[5]

Gosling, like so many other writers in the analytic and therapeutic world, wants to underline the problems that face us if we assume that the ideal relationship to our environment is control, moving towards a perfect static situation where we have nothing to lose, to fear or to gain. Behind all that is an impatience with the passage of time itself, which may well have become one of the factors of life in the developed modern world. Personal reality in the way I've been defining it unfolds itself and declares itself in *time* and in the *body*. Individualist awareness resents both time and body, resents unfinishedness, resents limitation.

Reclaiming the person

So we are in a cultural and work environment where it seems that individualist assumptions prevail, assumptions about control, assumptions about unavoidable conflict, assumptions about there being always a private area into which we can retreat and shut the doors. It is a culture in which all of those things work against what I began with as a personalist model. Yet Sennett can say, very importantly, towards the end of his book, that 'Cooperation is not like a hermetic object, once damaged beyond recovery; as we've seen, its sources – both genetic and in early human development – are instead enduring; they admit repair.'[6] If we live in an uncooperative environment, if we've developed uncooperative selves, the field is not lost. Something can be reclaimed. But it can be reclaimed only by a careful, systematic challenge to those assumptions about what the human is that so imprison us – a challenge to our (in the broader sense) educational philosophies. That's a challenge that needs clarity about what a person is and isn't; clarity about the difference between the person and the mere individual; clarity about the capacity of human agents to do what my sources describe as transcending the merely natural, transcending the simple list of things that happen to be true about me.

Such clarity is not easily available either for a simply *materialist* view of human life – the human individual as a machine (we touched on the problems raised by this sort of language in the first chapter of this book) – or for a purely *spiritualist* view of human life – human identity is just the sovereign iron will that lives somewhere in here and imposes itself on the world out there. Somewhere in between is an understanding of human identity, human personality, as fascinatingly and inescapably a hybrid reality: material, embedded in the material world, subject to the passage of time, and yet mysteriously able to respond to its environment so as to make a different environment; able to go beyond the agenda that is set, to reshape what is around; above all, committed to receiving and giving, to being dependent as well as independent, because that's what relation is. I am neither a machine nor a self-contained soul. I'm a person because I am spoken to, I'm attended to, and I'm spoken and attended and loved into actual existence. Which takes us back to the question of human

> There is always something about the other person that's to do with what I can't see, and that can't be mastered

dignity and the sacred, and to that pervasive, mysterious, nagging sense that there is always something about the other person that's to do with what I can't see and that can't be mastered.

But, finally, this is all a lot simpler than it sounds, because if we ask how we do, as a matter of fact, relate to one another, we may notice a number of things. We relate to one another as bodies. We notice that there is a fundamental bodily difference among human beings that has to do with gender, and we notice there's a fundamental bodily fact about us which is that our bodies wear out and that we're going to die. We talk to one another and we expect to listen to one another. We expect, in other words, relationship to evolve in language. We behave as if relationship mattered, as if we were not, in fact, capable of setting our own agenda for ever and a day. And when we encounter people who apparently don't behave like that we regard them as, to put it mildly, a bit problematic.

The question is, can we find a language for this simple everyday fact about us – that we speak and we listen, that we recognize our bodies and their difference and their vulnerability? Can we find a language for living that kind of life, because neither the 'machine' language nor the 'independent soul' language will do the job? We need a language of personhood. And Vladimir Lossky, with whom

I began, was quite right to say that it's really very difficult to get a clear *concept*, even if we do know what we're talking about.

But that does land us with the final and, I find, rather appealing paradox. People quite often say that theology is about describing unreal relations between unreal subjects; Friedrich Nietzsche said it famously in the nineteenth century and many have said it since. But what I'm really suggesting is that when it comes to personal reality the language of theology is possibly the *only* way to speak well of our sense of who we are and what our humanity is like – to speak well of ourselves as expecting relationship, as expecting difference, as expecting death. (And, of course, for Christians and people in other faith traditions, expecting rather more than death as well – but that's perhaps for another occasion.)

What I want to leave you with is simply the sense that it is in turning away from an atomized, artificial notion of the self as simply setting its own agenda from inside towards that more fluid, more risky, but also more human discourse of the exchanges in relations in which we're involved, and grounding that on the basic theological insight that we are always already in advance spoken to, addressed and engaged with by that which is not the world and not ourselves. It's in that process that theology comes into its own.

For reflection or discussion

1 What difference does it make to see yourself as a person rather than an individual?
2 Do you ever wish you felt more in control of others? Is that a good feeling to have?

3

Bodies, minds and thoughts

I referred earlier in this book to the work of Iain McGilchrist, whose enormous book *The Master and His Emissary* offers an analysis of the history of Western culture in the last few centuries, based on the assumption that we are seriously, if not dangerously, misunderstanding the nature of our whole mental life in our current culture.[1] *The Master and His Emissary* is written, as we noted earlier, by somebody who, unusually, is trained both in English literature and in neuroscience and has also been a practising therapist. The neuroscience enables him to write very intelligently about the ways in which the hemispheres of the brain operate; the English literature qualification enables him to think about the way the fiction, the poetry and the visual art of the last few hundred years suggest a gradual shift in how we think about thinking; and the therapist, of course, suggests some of what might need to be done about it. In a nutshell, for those of you who haven't come across this book, the thesis runs something like this.

While it's clearly an oversimplification to think that the two hemispheres of the brain work in isolation or in totally different ways, the fact remains that the two hemispheres privilege certain kinds of thinking, certain kinds of figuring and mapping of the world we're in. The left brain, which is generally the more analytic, the more pattern-making, the more problem-solving bit of the brain, is a crucial element in identifying on a fairly small scale what *specific* challenges face us and what *specific* responses are needed. It's reactive; it's something that breaks down into smaller rather than expanding to larger patterns, and so far as it goes it's one of the things that makes us the competent agents we are, people who know how to do things with things.

The two hemispheres of the brain . . . privilege certain kinds of thinking, certain kinds of figuring and mapping of the world we're in

The right brain, on the other hand, which is less associated with certain kinds of linguistic skills, builds larger models; it sees larger horizons, it makes connections that are not just argumentative or functional or practical. It scans the horizon, it risks putting phenomena together in what may be unexpected patterns. In certain ways, it's more patient of, more capable of working with, particular kinds of physical habit, and learning. When you're learning how to ride a bike or play a cello, it may be the right brain rather than the left that is more deeply engaged. In the ideal world, which we probably never occupied, the left brain is the 'emissary' in McGilchrist's terms: it does the routine work for the larger pattern-building enterprise of the right brain. But when things are going badly wrong, the left brain, the analytic and problem-solving side of us, takes over in ways that end up shrinking our horizons, reducing our capacity to formulate and understand the very problems that we're out to solve. And McGilchrist believes that it's this imbalance that we currently suffer from.

Thinking with our bodies

I am taking for granted some of that very ambitious, wide-ranging and broad-brush analysis in outlining my case in this chapter, because I want to reflect particularly not just on forms of knowing but on the role of the *body* in knowing. One of the things that the left brain can persuade us of is that knowing things is something that happens inside our heads. Inside our heads there is a highly developed lighthouse beam, invisible but none the less effective. It swivels around from this interior point and lights up problem after problem, situation after situation. It switches on its full strength and we then activate our capacity in order to solve the particular problem that is proposed to us, inside our heads. And what not only McGilchrist but a good many other philosophers and analysts of our contemporary cultural world – I think of the Canadian Philip Shepherd[2] here as well – have said is that this brackets out the actual process by which we learn to know most of what we know. This process of learning is something that we need to attend to if we're not to be stuck with a highly mythological and, at the end of the day, rather destructive model of what knowing is like. The lighthouse beam model will consistently persuade us to draw in our horizons, to concentrate on function rather than vision, and will therefore finally make us less recognizably human to one another than we might otherwise be.

Think for a moment of things that you have learned to know. I mentioned a moment ago riding bikes and playing cellos; you might also ask what it is like to learn a song. Learning how to ride a bicycle or how to sing a song is learning a *set of habits which your body activates*. You learn to respond or resonate to your environment in a particular way. You learn that if you lean over this way on a bicycle, you fall off. You learn, in all sorts of very elusive ways, that when you try to activate your vocal chords in this manner rather than that, the sound that comes out is not a sound that anybody wants to hear. You learn habits; you learn to accommodate yourselves to a complex set of stimuli which you probably couldn't ever tabulate in full. People who learn crafts learn very much in this way. They learn by imitation, they learn literally by feeling their way, and a book like Richard Sennett's *The Craftsman*[3] spells out something of what it means to learn a craft in ways in which he argues have very serious and very significant implications for the kind of humanity we grow into.

Learning a craft takes you time; it requires a forgetting of certain kinds of anxiety. You can't learn to be, let's say, a woodcarver if you're constantly anxious. Physical tension will be dangerous and destructive for you, and you will not produce what you are meant to be producing. You

Learning a craft takes you time; it requires a forgetting of certain kinds of anxiety

have, in other words, once again to learn habits, physical habits of unclenching; unclenching your attention and literally unclenching your muscles. And this issues in the making of knowledge, a practical knowledge of how to feel your way in the environment. It shouldn't surprise us, because that's how we begin to know anything, if you think about it. In the first chapter I mentioned the idea that we learn knowledge and language as small children as much as anything by the experience of bumping into things. We gradually map a physical environment in terms of where we go and where we can't go, where if we go we run into something and can't move on in a straight line. We create for ourselves a mental geography, bounded by those physical bits of resistance that gradually take a connected shape. To learn that somebody else is a body is literally learning our way around them. So, the level of learning that involves the body acquiring certain habits, and imagining certain perspectives (about which I'll say more in a moment), is where our human knowing most deeply belongs.

It is in the service of some of the specific challenges that arise as a result of this that the 'emissary', the left brain, begins its work. If I can't get round this particular obstacle, exactly why can't I, and how do I focus my attention in such a way that there will be a way of getting around it? Now, quite clearly, if we forget the process of our human learning, the way in which learning physical habits is deeply engrained in or embedded in the body, we will end up with a governing model of knowing, which, because it is analytical, is in danger of being disembodied, which is not any longer about feeling our way around. It will no doubt be highly effective in identifying *this* particular corner of the environment as requiring *this* particular set of strategies to get through it. But it won't tell us what the whole object is, the whole picture; it won't give us a map as such. And in neurological terms (as noted in Chapter 1) this has been illustrated with stark and painful clarity by the fact that certain kinds of brain lesion leave people with the capacity to recognize features but not faces: that is, people will know that that is a nose, but they will be unable to see whose face it is. This is quite a helpful metaphor for some of what's problematic in such a model of knowledge. Physical knowing becomes very literally a way of inhabiting an environment – that is, learning and knowing how to move around within it. Not everything reduces immediately to a problem, and the knowledge that I have is neither a knowledge of a set of facts nor simply a set of strategies. It's an acquaintance, a capacity to imagine, to create or postulate how the resistance that is around me actually looks overall.

Without that capacity, our concept of what's human, and thus our concept of our entire culture, thins out dramatically. The case made by McGilchrist, Shepherd and others is that this 'thinning out' is not only about a kind of incompetence at building larger pictures of our physical environment, but also has to do with problems in building larger pictures of our emotional environment. The more we are fixated on problem-solving, the more we are fixated upon control, the more lack of control and frustration at failure to solve problems create personal challenges for us, and the more we're inclined to lash out. There is a fair bit of evidence from the neurological world about the connections between violence, obsession and control; even more broadly, if a little less poisonously, we can say that it issues in an impatience with taking time over anything. That may sound faintly familiar as a portrait of cultures that you and I have no doubt inhabited with some regularity. But I think that it's possible to map all of this on to some aspects of our social, cultural and indeed political world at the moment in ways that may be illuminating.

We are notoriously subject to short attention spans in contemporary culture – and I don't just mean the average length of an episode of a television drama. I mean also the average length of time that a story lasts in the media, or indeed the average reach that a declaration of government policy may envisage. We are short-termist, almost by compulsion, these days. We're encouraged to assume that the solving of the problem immediately in front of us is what matters, and we lose track of the larger questions about the meaning of our social institutions, the purpose of our social institutions in the long term, and equally impatient of understanding exactly how we got here. One of the most interesting and troubling things about our contemporary culture is a point that was flagged up a few years ago in a very interesting document by Jo Guldi and David Armitage, *The History Manifesto*,[4] which spoke about the way in which the 'thinning out' of historical knowledge in general, not least, alas, in some institutions of higher education, meant that we were now impatient to understand how we got to where we are. But if we don't know how we got here,

If we don't know how we got here, we will tend to assume that where we are is obvious

we will tend to assume that where we are is obvious. If we assume that where we are is obvious, we are less likely to ask critical questions about it. The less likely we are to ask critical questions about it, the more resistant we will be to other people's challenges to it. In other words, not understanding how we learned to be the people we now are has an immediate and highly dangerous effect on the kind of society we are and might seek to be, just as it might have a dangerous effect on any individual who tries to block out the memory of the experiences that have, as a matter of fact, made them who they are.

So we're not just talking about philosophical theory here, we are talking about attitudes to knowing and learning which have some measureable effect, some measurable significance, for the sort of society we are, and think we are, and might want to be, for where we might be going, for what we take for granted. But there is one more point before I move on, about minds and bodies. I've emphasized so far how very important it is that we understand a great deal of our habitual learning in terms of the body acquiring the habits it needs to move around in an environment without bumping into too many things; how the acquiring of habits, of feeling, sensing, participating, is crucial to growing in knowledge. The other side of this coin is that the body itself becomes something much more deeply imbued with the mind. If the mind is emphatically something we learn about *as bodies*, the very notion of the body takes for granted something about the mind. In Chapter 1 I mentioned Edith Stein, who was the first to remark that it's philosophically interesting that we can't see the backs of our heads. That's to say, she argued that for us to have an image of ourselves as a body, as a three-dimensional unit in space, requires us to listen to and attend to what other people are doing with respect to us. There's something the other knows that I *absolutely* can't; that is, what the back of my head looks like 'head on', so to speak. Expand that in various ways and you see how it applies in the construction of a *physical* picture of myself – but also in certain aspects of the construction of a mental or psychological picture of myself: I cannot know myself alone. I cannot invent language for myself: I have to be spoken *to*. I cannot picture myself as a body or a self unless I am seen and engaged *with*. And, in that sense, Stein claims that aspects of empathy are essential to our processes of knowing.[5]

Empathy, that is, the imaginative identification with a perspective that is not my own, is not just an optional extra in our human identity and our human repertoire, it's something without which we cannot know ourselves. Without identification with the other, I don't know myself.

To think of body without the engagement and the exchange of intelligent subjects, without the imaginative projection of self into the other, is not possible. Our knowing, in other words, is not *only* bodily, it's also cooperative and imaginative. Going back to the 'lighthouse in the brain' model, the problem with this is not only that it is dangerously on the way to being disembodied, it is also highly individualized. And if we

Without identification with the other, I don't know myself

want to redress the balance in certain ways of thinking how we know, and what it is to know, we will need not only to reinstate the connectedness of body and mind, but to find something interesting to say about the cooperative character of the enterprise of knowing itself.

Developing practical intelligence

To move on a little: knowledge understood in these terms of relatedness to body and interchange and language appears to be less about fixing on the identifying of an object that can be analysed exhaustively, and (so to speak) absorbed into the knower, and more to do with (a favourite metaphor of mine) 'attunement', being on a wavelength, being aware that there are stimuli coming into us to which, as embodied minds or intelligent bodies, we are learning to vibrate. If I were being a little bit too epigrammatic for my own good, I would suggest that perhaps knowledge in this connection involves *attention, attunement and atonement*. It involves a highly developed capacity to be absorbed by, not just to absorb, attention. It requires an awareness of how we resonate with and adjust to the stimuli that are coming into us as bodies, as intelligent bodies: attunement. It requires, finally, 'atonement', that is, the capacity to be, in some important sense, *at one* with environment and stimuli, agenda, suggestion, and all the rest. Only such a bundle of skills (or indeed, you might say, graces) amounts to real practical intelligence.

There are two subsidiary questions, of interest both to someone with a theological and to someone with an academic slant. Let's take the academic example first. In our teaching at every level, what are the kinds of knowledge we privilege, what are the kinds of knowledge we seek to nurture and encourage and develop, and how far do our institutions allow us to have the 'binocular vision', both hemispheres of the brain, that we need in order to be intelligent? Many of my own teaching colleagues have voiced the anxiety that certain models of knowledge – analytic, short-term, binary and problem-solving – are in many areas elbowing out certain other kinds – models of attunement or even atonement, as well as certain kinds of attentiveness.

I think it's a fair complaint, and a complaint that does indeed go all the way through the education system. We've been familiar for decades with a number of experiments in educational methods that have reminded us that there are other kinds of approach to the education of primary school age children than simply a set of easily checkable skills acquired in strict succession and tested relentlessly. Whether in Steiner or in Montessori schools, or simply in ordinary schools that have learned certain lessons, there's been an awareness that to nurture children in intelligence (in the sense in which I've been using the word) requires more consideration than is usually given to *how the body works intelligently*, to the embodied mind, in fact. Which is why play, music, sport, leisure, drama all have so crucial a role in the formation of the intelligent child. And while most primary schools in our country hold on to some version of that, it's interesting and rather puzzling that these things are clearly seen as less worth attending to once a child is 11 years old. From that point on, it appears that other models of knowledge increasingly predominate – and predominate in a way that has led us for quite a long time (though let's not idealize the past here) to undervalue and disvalue those elements of craft learning that require sophistication of intelligence, patience and, dare I say it, spiritual maturity. The demise of apprenticeships in British education is not just a casual, regrettable fact about the way in which industry works; I suspect it also has something to say about what kind of learning we think really *counts*. There is a good deal more that could be said about the education establishment and the educational philosophy we are currently used to, but I think the point is fairly made. I want to go on to say a little bit about the theological implications as well.

To turn to what may seem a rather unlikely locus for thinking about these subjects, the writings of St Augustine, one of the most interesting bits of argumentation in his autobiographical reflections in the *Confessions* has to do with knowledge and learning. He describes famously in the seventh book of his *Confessions*[6] how he struggled to attain spiritual knowledge: how he followed sacrificially and devotedly a path of mental abstraction and inwardness to put him in touch with eternal verities; and he describes how that didn't quite seem to work in breaking his habits, in changing his life, in acquainting him with a living truth such as he was seeking. He uses an extraordinarily powerful image in Book VII of how, frustrated and pained by his failure in connecting up his ordinary, daily life with the experience of mental abstraction and elevated contemplation, he finally gave himself up to the Christian faith, throwing himself down, he says, on the embodied divinity that was stretched out at his feet – the human narrative of Jesus Christ. For Augustine, the way up is the way down. That is to say, learning anything about the spirit, the spiritual realm, let alone God, involves a way down. It involves a recognition of one's own mortality and physicality; it involves – for him specifically as a Christian – the recognition that God has spoken and acted in a very particular social, historical and material context: that is, in the life of Jesus. And this image of throwing oneself down, in order, as Augustine says, that we may rise with the rising of Christ, is not a bad metaphor for some of what we have been thinking about in this chapter.

It's a helpful metaphor not least because it's about the way in which our human mental processes, and spiritual processes, are perpetually seduced by the model of *escape* and the model of *control*. Mysteriously, we as human beings would quite like not to be material a lot of the time. And, at its most marked, we see this in what we've learnt to call the 'transhumanist' philosophy, which imagines what it might be like for us to be, if not literally 'brains in a vat' at least something rather like that, with the emotional and cognitive content of our systems being transferrable from container to container – and therefore guaranteed an immortality of some kind. Whether this is more than science fiction is debatable; but whether or not it's science fiction, the aspiration, the dream of liberty from the body, is an intriguing and puzzling one in our history. And, as I say, lest we imagine that somewhere

> *Mysteriously, we as human beings would quite like not to be material a lot of the time*

there was a golden age of integration, it's a dream whose roots are very deep in our past as a culture: as a Christian culture, as a Platonic culture, as a classical culture. It is undoubtedly a significant European and North Atlantic problem, but hardly one confined to a single area of our world.

But if the sketch that I've offered is in anything like the right territory, then there is something about our embodiedness and about the kinds of exchange that bodies have that is intrinsic to intelligence itself – or at least to put it a little less loadedly, what we have to mean by intelligence would have to be very different if it were not involved in the exchange, confrontation and encounter of bodies, and therefore with the taking of time. The dream so often seems to reduce to that persistent aspiration that there could be ways of knowledge, ways of knowing, ways of mastery, which didn't depend on the contingency of taking time, on the labour of finding one's way around, and indeed therefore on the difficulty of inhabiting our environment.

That's one of the last points I want to underline here: difficulty. I think difficulty is good for us, and I say that not just as an excuse for writing some of the books I've written, which I'm told are not always easy reading. I say it because difficulty is one of those things that, rather obviously, obliges us to take time. The more time we take, the more our discovery is likely to turn into habit and into inhabiting. The less time we take over something, the easier we find something to resolve, map and digest, the less value, the less significance it will have. It's a rather old chestnut: Platonic philosophers and early Christian theologians were saying millennia back that the more easily you thought you'd got to know something, the less you'd care about it. Difficulty imposes discipline: it imposes the willingness to believe that there is more to work on. And by reminding us that getting to where we are has taken time, it can also be one of the things that reminds us that our current cultural perspective, temporal or geographical, is not the only obvious one. Taking time, the awareness of the 'more' that we have not yet absorbed, may be one of the things (may be, it doesn't have to be) making us that little bit more patient with the criticism, the challenge, the alternative view, of another world, another culture, another person. It may be one of those things that builds *solidarity* rather than division, something, in other words, that extends the cooperation that properly belongs to knowledge.

Once again, there's a theological flicker in the background, to do with the relationship between knowledge and communion. But it is enough for now just to underline the initial positive significance of difficulty. We need in our inhabiting of the world to take very seriously the fact that the world resists being controlled and digested by human subjects. We repeatedly act as if control and digestion were the only things that mattered; and this of course explains a lot about the ecological crisis that we currently face. But if we return to the centrality of time and difficulty and embodied labour, there is really no way round grasping the fact that we as bodies belong in a world where bodily processes connect us to a material world to which we are not superior. This in itself imposes on us a more patient, a more attentive, perhaps even more 'reverent' approach to the environment we live in. There's no great novelty in making the point, but it may as well be made: how we think knowledge works affects how we approach our environment. If our model of knowledge is the lighthouse in the brain, there is that much more risk of supposing that the knowing subject is so very different from anything out there to be known, that there is a fixed gulf between the human and the non-human: and this is surely one of the things that we are having to learn to go beyond in our inhabiting of a world of limited resources and increasing instability.

> *We need in our inhabiting of the world to take very seriously the fact that the world resists being controlled and digested by human subjects*

Think of the tree of the knowledge of good and evil in the Garden of Eden. It's intriguing that when people talk about neurophysiology they talk, among other things, about 'dendritic' elements in the brain – tree-like elements, the proliferation and spreading of antennae within particular neuron structures. It's interesting too that the notion of trees with crowns above the ground and roots beneath has again and again returned as a metaphor for what we know we know and what we don't know we know; and it's interesting that a late classical philosopher like Porphyry could catalogue the variants of logical method using the metaphor of a tree. There is, it seems, something about the organic life of a tree that compulsively draws or attracts to itself thinking about knowledge. And to think about knowledge in terms of that above- and below-ground model – what we know we know, what we think we know, and what we don't know we know – is not only a helpful but perhaps even a saving reminder of the risk of reducing what we mean by knowledge to a certain set of skills and capacities; the risk of forgetting that what we know comes from *where* we are, and where we are takes *time* to get to; the risk of failing to inhabit our world, and thus to inhabit our bodies. As I've suggested, the risk involved here is not simply the risk of a worrying philosophical mistake, but something like the risk of losing what it might mean to be human at all.

For reflection or discussion

1 Can you think of something you know how to do requiring a skill that took time to develop? How did you learn
that skill and develop that knowledge? Are there other
areas of your life that might be developed in a similar
way?

2 What is empathy, how is it developed and why is it so
essential to being human?

4

Faith and human flourishing

Religion today is often understood, from within and without, as having a lot to do with what moral philosophers call 'heteronomy' – that is, the imposition of law, convention, norms from outside, from the 'other'. Religious identity is seen as inevitably allied, to a greater or lesser degree, with repression. To be religious, on this account, is to be subject to the will of a divine power, and therefore to be called upon to make dramatic and consistent self-sacrifice. There's no need for me to elaborate the ways in which such a model has been abused, distorted and used for anti-human purposes across the centuries. The point is that if that account is correct, if that is what religious identity *is* about, then the two items in my title, faith and human flourishing, don't very easily belong together. If, on the other hand, we conceive of divine power as an absolute freedom to bring the other into being, without fear, rivalry or anxiety, then that would in turn suggest a different way of understanding human maturity and flourishing. I'm therefore going to suggest four lines of enquiry here, four themes that might help us develop a definition of human maturity

69

religiously informed. The themes are these: how we handle dependence and autonomy; the education of passion; the taking of time; and the acceptance of mortality.

Dependence and autonomy

Autonomy is very much an accepted ideal of modern and late-modern culture; and it's perhaps a little bit too much of a cliché (though you often hear it from some religious people) to say that it's a mistake to regard autonomy as a supreme human value. I don't want to simplify this unduly, but I do think that there are issues in how we talk about, how we understand, autonomy. Dependence is, after all, a condition of human life in certain phases and circumstances, importantly inescapable for us. The long latency period of the human young, the phenomenon of language, the relative physical vulnerability of the human organism in its environment, all of these things build in to our distinctive human experience a dimension of inescapable *receiving*, formation-by. To suppose that we are our own authors is to try and escape from some of these dimensions of our humanity. Negotiating what it means to be dependent is part of being human. The moral problem that has always surrounded this has

> *Negotiating what it means to be dependent is part of being human*

70

been that very often, when people talk about the need to accept dependence, they mean 'you need to accept your dependence on me', or some equivalent of that. That is to say, it's about inequality, imbalance within the human world.

But this doesn't absolve us from trying to make sense of what it is to be receivers as well as creators. What some have called 'the illusion of self-creation' is a serious and vexing problem in how we understand the development of the human psyche. A generation or so ago, that remarkable and rather controversial writer Ernest Becker wrote extensively about what he called 'the project of self-creation', and how, prolonged beyond a certain developmental stage, it becomes the source of all kinds of pathologies. He quotes Søren Kierkegaard's definition of demoniac rage, an attack on all of life for what it has dared to do to one' as a manifestation of 'defiant self-creation'[1] – the anger of the would-be self-creator, when the world of the self proves not, after all, to be under the control of the will. Now, to generalize wildly for a moment, the position of most religious faith is that all of us share one fundamental form of dependence, which is our dependence on divine liberty. We are here because there is an act that we echo, participate in, reflect – however you want to put it – an act of initiative in virtue of which we are here at all. And so for us to

71

Passions disciplined by the Law of God

be ourselves, the acknowledgement of that level of dependence is, very importantly, part of what sets us free because it acquaints us with what is *true* about us; we depend on what is not ours, what is not us, our will, our hope, our achievement.

In its Christian version, this has a very specific colouring. Christians are encouraged to think of themselves as growing into not simply 'the divine life' in general terms, but into the particular form of divine life represented by the 'Word', the 'Son', the offspring of the eternal source. Christians are adopted into a dependent relationship to that which Jesus calls '*Abba*, Father'. Our human identity therefore becomes one in which we both acknowledge in prayer this dependence and respond to the gift that sets up not only our being but our renewed being in Christ; and in acknowledging that dependence we are empowered to 'do the work of God', to be 'in Christ', as St Paul puts it. It's about an authority that emerges from yielding not to an alien will but to an affirming source – recognizing that we are here because there is an act that draws us into being and affirms our being. So we do not have to be our own origin; we do not have to try to be self-creators. There is a level of affirmation bringing us into, and holding us in existence, which we do not have to work for.

In this first area of handling dependence and autonomy, one of the proposals of religious faith and religious language is that we are empowered, emancipated, to use the transforming energy we can exercise by acknowledging our dependence on an unconditional source of affirmation. I have given the version of this which is particularly associated with Christian language and Christian doctrine; we could spend longer on what that means in other religious contexts, but the theme in various guises runs across confessional boundaries to a significant degree. (I'm not, I should also add, suggesting that 'all religions are saying the same thing', only attempting to note and tease out some of those things that characterize a religious form of identity or self-understanding overall in the story of human culture.)

The education of passion

I come now to my second overarching theme. 'Passion', in both Christian and Buddhist usage, has some very specific associations; it's not simply a matter of emotions or instinct. The passions, as analysed and discussed particularly in the ascetical literature of the fourth to the eighth century in the Christian world (and indeed for much longer in the Eastern Christian world), are those disturbances of the proper or fruitful condition of the self associated with inappropriate response to outside stimuli. Prodded and stimulated into life by the environment we're in, we can, says the great Evagrius, at the end of the fourth century, respond in a variety of ways; some human, some diabolical and some angelic or divine: a human response, pragmatic and exploratory; a diabolical response, which seeks to master an environment and turn it solely to the purposes of the ego; a healed and redeemed response, which regards what is around us in its own right, in its own dignity, not seeking to make it serve our private ends. Passion is the diabolical response; it is that response to an environment that is concerned simply to own and absorb, that is incapable of seeing what *is*, in its own right, in its own dimensionality.

There are several ways in which uneducated passion can confirm our 'unfreedom', our moral and spiritual slavery. It is quite tempting to lift from our shoulders the burden of intelligent choice by naturalizing our motivations, by saying, 'These are the impulses I have, and therefore they need to be fulfilled. I don't need to reflect on them, assess them, discern them, choose between them, there they are.' Lifting the burden of choice by appeal to an unexamined instinctual life is one of the obvious temptations we face there, and it can find its more contemporary forms in various types of neurological determinism: 'I don't really choose, this is what happens in me. I don't act, things happen.' But just as with unexamined, uncriticized passion, to assume this absolute given-ness of our needs and desires lends us a solid, self-oriented agenda which potentially has to be defended against others.

If I had to try to sum up what the word 'passion' means in the classical Christian tradition, it seems to me to designate two things: the uncritical affirmation of the ego, and the positioning of that ego in a state of struggle and rivalry. Major religious traditions – particularly Buddhism and Christianity – offer both a diagnosis of passion and a pedagogy, a way of educating passion, not simply eradicating but understanding. And such understanding has a lot to do with discerning what this life of passion (serves) what its goals and products are. So by putting our reflex, 'passionate' responses to the world under scrutiny we may find what it is that those reflexes are aiming at, and thus perhaps understand better how to reroute some of their energy away from the world of contest, struggle and rivalry.

Passion means the uncritical affirmation of the ego, and the positioning of that ego in a state of struggle and rivalry

When Christians, in that classical period of spiritual reflection between the fourth and the eighth century, talked about *apatheia* as the Christian ideal, they emphatically did not mean 'apathy'; they didn't even mean the total absence of the instinctual life as such. They were thinking of that state in which you are aware of

75

you can't control – don't let passions

your reflexes and responses in such a way that you can think through them, sense your way towards a goal that is not purely self-protective or acquisitive. There is a good deal in the tradition about the proper use of passion, sometimes to undercut other sorts of passion. You can find there are some responses whose undue energy or even relative violence can be deployed to knock other selfish, instinctual behaviours off course. But that's to go into more detail than is required here. The point is: there is a diagnosis, there is a pedagogy. There is a possibility of being aware of how one responds in the environment, and the possibility of intelligently reshaping that response.

Turn to the Buddhist thought world and of course the categories are dramatically different – and yet some of the same issues can be identified. For the Buddhist, release comes when you recognize the totally conditioned character not only of your responses but of *every* act, mental and physical, in which you are involved. The beginning of wisdom is to dissolve the solidity of self-feeding speech and thought, in order to create a different kind of space within the world, which, in at least some traditions of Buddhism, shows itself in what we call compassion. The scrutiny and education of the passions becomes a second area in which religious identity has something distinct to say about human identity; in which it appears as a distinct form of human identity characterized by practices and images, rooted in specific and diverse narratives, that nonetheless have cross-cultural parallels in the way that they work.

Taking time

My third area may be rather less obvious. I want to suggest that attitudes to *time*, and the passage of time, are deeply characteristic of distinctively religious behaviour. People of faith do things with the calendar. As you know, one of the easiest default settings if in doubt as to what to teach in religious education in schools is to teach children about festivals. And although that can sometimes be anecdotal and unhelpful, the instinct behind it is not completely faulty. How religious communities spend their time is a serious and central theme. Time is not undifferentiated; its passing is marked in ways that are thought to be significant. So the passage of time becomes not just a trajectory of acquisition (acquiring property, acquiring power, acquiring security); it comes to be about the repeated accumulation, as you might say, of meaning, returning to symbolic resources to rediscover aspects of the universe you inhabit, aspects of yourself; to reconnect specific ongoing experience with steady, regular or rhythmical patterns, laid out in the language and practice of a religious community. You keep going back to the practices, the stories, in celebration and commemoration. Time, therefore, becomes neither simply cyclical nor simply linear. It moves, you change; at the same time there is something to which you *return*, to rediscover and enlarge the understanding acquired in the passage of time. And all of that adds up to dissolving any idea that time is a limited commodity (or indeed any kind of commodity) that has to be squeezed as hard as possible in order to keep the trajectory of acquisition going. Time is a complex and rich gift; it is the medium in which we not only grow and move forward but also constructively return and resource – literally re-source – ourselves.

> *Time is a complex and rich gift; it is the medium in which we not only grow and move forward but also constructively return and resource – literally re-source – ourselves*

There are deep implications within that for how we approach human work and human well-being, and how we understand and how we cultivate a fruitful rhythm in action and human engagement. Increasingly, one of the marks of a fully and uncompromisingly secular environment is the notion of undifferentiated time. There are, for mature late capitalism, no such things as weekends. The problem with this kind of secularism is not so much a denial of the existence of God as the denial of the possibility of leisure – of time that is not spent in serving the market. That is to say, for a particular mind-set, acquisitive and purpose-driven, the passage of time is precisely the slipping away of a scarce, valuable commodity, every moment of which has to be made to yield its maximum possible result, so you can't afford to stop. This kind of secular understanding of the passage of time is perhaps one of those areas where there is most open collision between the fundamentally religious and the fundamentally anti-religious mindset – and I think that's one of the untold stories of our time. We imagine, quite often, that the really fundamental collisions are around metaphysics or ethics. But perhaps there's another area at least as important, which is how we approach the time we are in, the time we spend – and, indeed, the time we 'waste'.

Accepting our mortality

The three themes we've thought about so far – the struggle for autonomy, the seduction of unexamined or uncriticized passion, and our desperation about time – converge with the deepest question of all, that of our anxiety about death and our reluctance to accept mortality.

The fact of our mortality means that *every* project we have is limited. There is something non-negotiable about that absolute limit, and there is an ultimate challenge in that to any fantasy or fiction of the all-powerful ego. It is resistance to mortality – 'the denial of death', in the title of Ernest Becker's best-known book – that takes us into the worst pathologies of power, the imagined power to rebel against the ultimate limit, the fact that we are going to die.[2] The knowledge of mortality runs through all the other themes we have considered in one way or another, because the denial of the knowledge of mortality returns us to false, destructive models of power. The characteristically religious response includes a balance of attention to the immediate and resignation to the long-term. 'Redeem thy misspent time that's past, Live this day as if 'twere thy last', says the Anglican hymn.[3] That is to say, attention to what's immediately to be done, along with acceptance of long-term limit and finitude, is what we're asked to grow into and to engage in. It's not about a wavering level of attention to the present for the sake of an imagined future (though that's the way it's sometimes been treated: 'We're going to die so we'd better have a plan' is not quite what this is about . . .).

To summarize the four themes we've been exploring in this chapter: we've thought about how being a mature human is shaped by an acceptance of a liberty on which we depend, by embracing the need for honesty and discipline in our instinctual life, by a readiness to see the passage of time as symbolic and complex (not just an undifferentiated continuum that has to be filled), and by a recognition of the ultimate limit imposed by mortality. Non-disabling dependence, a freedom for self-critique, patience and literacy in ritual, and lack of anxiety in the face of death – the absence of any or all of these can contribute to dysfunction in human communities, and dysfunctional human individuals, those who are rebelling against any form of dependence, those who cannot cope with the notion of self-question or self-critique, those who wish to treat time as something that has to be filled up, those who are in denial of their mortality. But, having said all that, those four crucial 'seasons' of the life of the spirit are all of them capable of being distorted and misrepresented within the religious idiom, within the religious rhetoric and system. If we're going to talk about those four as positive things, it's important to be aware of the negativity that can also be triggered.

To put it another way, what I called 'non-disabling dependence' can be replaced by infantilism, by love of dependence for its own sake, divorced from any notion that dependence enables or liberates. Institutions and authorities, religious institutes and authorities, are (in case you haven't noticed) capable of very high degrees of infantilization of communities; and sometimes that is welcome

81

" Receivers "

Void filled
by " Dad "
thing

to those for whom non-disabling dependence is rather hard work (which accounts for most of us, most of the time).

Again, instead of the critical and constructive approach to passion suggested by aspects of the classical tradition, we can take refuge in emotional repression. We can elevate the will over the feelings – which is empathetically not what the classical discussion of passion is about – in the hope that, somehow dangerous, uncontrollable or unpredictable instincts can be controlled by our decision.

We can turn the creative and constructive use of the rituals of time into ritualism and the fear of change, instead of a sense of the sacredness of a time that is given to us for constant, cumulative rediscovery.

And, of course, religious language is more than capable of renewing and intensifying anxiety in the face of death, partly by certain kinds of talk about divine judgement – you have every reason to be afraid of death because of what's coming after; or it can encourage you to ignore the present for the sake of an imagined future of consolation and vindication in the distance beyond actual human pressures and decisions.

All of these aspects of religiously shaped human flourishing that we have considered are capable of being, in effect, turned on their heads and distorted in ways like those. And if we are to avoid that kind of distortion, that kind of turning upside down of what I believe to be the essentially constructive and flourishing models I've been trying to outline, we need to reflect on the central meaning of human dependency on God, and how dependence on *God* is radically unlike yielding to someone else who is like you. Depending on God is utterly unlike losing a struggle for power, losing your control, losing your autonomy. To be unconditionally dependent on another human subject is to be in deep danger of repressive, dehumanizing patterns of relation. To depend on God in the context I have outlined is precisely to be delivered from this. God is not another ego greedy to control. Likewise, freedom from passion, *apatheia*, is not giving up what is natural for the sake of the 'supernatural', but learning a perspective on oneself, learning the right and wrong exercises of the will in this, identifying some of the ways in which self-oriented responses to the world prevent us seeing what is there, and so allowing our vision to be cleansed, and our possibilities of action and relation to be changed and enlarged.

Getting our perspectives a little clearer on the 'grammar' of God, how we talk about God *as God*, is not only to do with clarifying and purifying what we say about God, it is also, crucially, a purifying of what we say about ourselves. To see oneself afresh in this light and to learn the grammar of talk about God belong absolutely and inseparably together. So if we are to recover any sense of religious commitment being more than just having a set of mental positions – usually seen as 'irrational' mental positions – we need to refocus a bit on how religious people speak of human flourishing. What is the 'human face' that is being uncovered in the practices of faith? It's a question increasingly posed about the habits of our contemporary world. Sennett's important work on the human psychological effects of capitalism has posed the question, 'What kind of human being does current global market practice presuppose, and what kind of human being does it nurture?' adding, 'Is this the sort of human being we want to be caught in a train carriage with?'[4] But the question is the same for any religious practice, habit or system: what kind of human face is being uncovered? What sort of humanity is being educated, nourished, developed, in this context, by this language?

It is very important for people of any faith to know what they look like in the eyes of others

This is where the criticism of religion by those who don't share its commitments is of such essential importance. Quite simply, it is very important for people of any faith to know what they look like in the eyes of others. Theirs may not be a fair, reasonable or comprehensive picture, but it is important to see what 'face' is actually being uncovered in the practices of faith, rather than simply hoping for the best. This exercise, this challenge, of trying to see what a mature human subject might look like who has been shaped by this style of living, thinking and imagining becomes a crucial focus of energy and reflection both for the well-being of religious communities and for the well-being of the human community (I suspect that people of faith don't often enough ask with seriousness the question, 'What does *our* humanity look like?') even if we repeatedly fail to wait long enough for the answer.

In this chapter I have been trying to put before you some of those things that I believe make for human flourishing, in the fullest sense, that are nourished, encouraged and enabled by certain assumptions in faith. I said earlier that I didn't want to go down the road of saying 'all faiths are saying the same thing'; there *are* ineradicable doctrinal disagreements that can't be glossed over, there are forms of cultural embeddedness that we can't ignore – and yet I believe there is something to be said for a dialogue among faiths that works hard at the processes of human formation, asking together about the kind of human face that the habits of faith uncover.

For reflection or discussion

1 What is your attitude to time? What are the positive and humanly constructive ways in which you might use it?

2 If you are a Christian, do you have any sense of how your faith and the way you practise it appear to people of other faiths?

See of VA –
Defend confederacy?

Role of Anglicans → cant look away
Evangelicals → lost sight?
Apostles Creed

5

Silence and human maturity

Dangerous it were for the feeble brain of man to wade far into the doings of the Most High, whom although to know be life and joy to make mention of His name, yet our soundest knowledge is to know that we know Him not as indeed He is, neither can know Him, and our safest eloquence concerning Him is our silence. He is above and we upon earth, therefore it behoveth our words to be wary and few. (Richard Hooker)[1]

It always feels strange to be talking about silence. It seems ironic to talk about it. We're stuck before we start. And that is quite a good place to begin; to know from the word go that *talking* about silence is a slightly silly thing to do puts words into perspective. The very oddity of trying to talk about silence reminds you what the relationship between one and the other is. So I say that as a kind of general health warning about what I'm going to discuss in this chapter. I want to think about where and how we encounter silence in our ordinary lives, what the significance of some of those encounters is, and how they connect with some of the ways in which silence appears to us in Scripture and in story. Perhaps out of that a few cautious thoughts may emerge about how we move more deeply into it.

When silence takes over

I begin with three experiences in which silence overtakes us. One of them is rather comical, one of them is not at all comical, and one of them is somewhere between. At some point, we've all had somebody say to us, 'Just tell me what's on your mind' – or worse still, 'Just be yourself'; and one quite common response to this is complete inarticulacy. 'Just tell me what's on your mind' is a suggestion that fails conspicuously to open things up. And as for 'Just be yourself', so often given as good advice to people before interviews or stressful events, I can hardly think of anything more calculated to double or treble the stress involved. It was the Roman Catholic scholar and essayist Ronald Knox who said that when somebody on one occasion had told him to 'pull himself together' his response was, 'I'm not sure I have a together.' And similarly, when someone tells you to be yourself, the problem is, 'Well, what's the self I "just have" to be?' That's one experience in which silence seems to overtake us.

There's another which is a lot less trivial but no less common: the silence that comes after 'The tests are positive', or whatever phrase you might associate with that. Something unmanageably tragic, unmanageably disruptive of ordinary life: it may be the announcement of a potentially fatal disease; or, more simply, a friend on the telephone saying that they're divorcing; it may be looking at the images that flood our screens and our newspapers of trauma and nightmare elsewhere in the world. It's the silence that comes not with our inability to express ourselves, our 'real selves', but our inability to know how to *react* at all to a reality that seems completely out of control.

Then there's a third kind of silence which always intrigues me, the silence at the end of a really good play or concert, the pause before the applause starts. Most of you will have experienced something of that. You watch Simon Russell Beale playing King Lear at the National Theatre, or go to a rather routine performance of a concert in the church hall, and there's something about it that at the very end says, 'I mustn't wrap this up too quickly. Let's give that little bit of extra space to allow it to be what it is and not rush to react.' So there's a silence, and then sooner or later some brave person (or somebody that the director or conductor has prompted) starts clapping, and, with a little bit of relief, something like normality resumes.

What all these experiences have in common is, I suggest, that they challenge our urge to get on top of situations, to control. One obvious way in which we try to get on top of situations is by talking. We all know that the sort of stressful experience that I spoke about at the beginning

('Tell me', 'Be yourself'), while it may produce silence, can also in some people produce an endless flow of chatter. We conquer the challenge of a situation by speech. And when we are in one way or another knocked sideways, displaced, wrong-footed by something we encounter, how very difficult it is to say, 'I can't domesticate this, I can't get it into a tidy form.' Silence is something to do with acknowledging a lack of power. I'll come back to that in a moment because it's quite a complex idea in itself.

Silence is something to do with acknowledging a lack of power

But you could put it in another way, by saying, 'There's no way of confidently absorbing or normalizing this experience.' Thinking back to the news in the hospital waiting room or the doctor's surgery, how do I *normalize* the knowledge that I'm going to die, or that someone I love is going to die? And when I've been taken into places I didn't know I had in me at the end of a really serious play or concert, again I feel I can't *normalize* this, I can't just absorb it into my routine ways of being in the world; I've been taken outside my comfort zone, I've been stripped of the ways in which I usually defend myself and organize the world I'm in. I'm left – as St John of the Cross once famously said – 'suspenso en el aire', 'suspended in the air',[2] or, as we might say in colloquial English, 'hung out to dry'. There's no way of making the otherness of this moment domestic, no way of just taking it into myself. And that's why I believe these moments of silence, silence imposing itself on us, are so very important not only for our humanity generally but for our Christian humanity in particular. They're important for our humanity in general because we habitually live in a world where the 'right thing' to do with critical moments is to stop them being critical. The right thing to do with a wild animal is to tame it, so to speak, and the right thing to do with any 'wild' experience is to work out what I can do with it, what I can make of it, and, in short, domesticate it.

Silence and human growth

But the more our humanity falls in love with this strange idea of domesticating, absorbing and controlling, the less human we actually get. I would venture to guess that the people we would least like to spend a long time with are people who have answers to every question and plans for every contingency. There's something slightly inhuman about that, because if we believe that our humanity is something constantly growing, then there have got to be moments when we are taken beyond the familiar and the controllable. A growing humanity, a maturing humanity, is one that's prepared for silence, because it's prepared at important moments to say, 'I can't domesticate, I can't get on top of this.' And of course it's hard work. I'm sure I'm not the only person who's been on silent retreats where you watch either yourself or somebody else in a group gradually becoming more and more alarmed that there is nothing they can say to make this 'normal'. (I remember a retreat where one unfortunate member of the group couldn't cope with silent meals; he'd bolt a mouthful of food, staring wildly around him, and then run from the room.) There's something so alarming about not being able to make this ordinary. And yet for us to grow, we need to learn how to cope with the *extra*-ordinary and to be ready all the time to keep moving. And this is just what you have to say about humanity in general, never mind what you have to say about the life of faith – because surely the life of faith, if it is anything, is a life in which we are, usually rather reluctantly, becoming extraordinary.

We all know that Christians are often very extraordinary people, in a none too complimentary sense; but the point is that the bare prose of our humanity is, by God, turned into poetry by that constant urging to grow. God is that environment, that encounter, that we will never get to the bottom of and that we will never control, and that, try as we may, we will never absorb, because God is God and we are what God makes and loves and works on. So to understand that there's something about silence that is profoundly at the

> The bare prose of our humanity is, by God, turned into poetry

92

heart of being human just begins to open up the recognition that being Christian requires us more than ever to come to terms with those moments when silence is imposed on us, when we face what we can't control.

It isn't surprising that people feel fear when they encounter silence. It's strange that often the older and more experienced and apparently mature we get, the harder silence can be. I have been struck more than once by the experience of taking part in meditation groups for primary school children, because the one thing they don't seem to feel is fear of silence. They may find it difficult in various ways, but I don't hear them talking about fear. Whereas so often for those of us older and wiser, this may be one of the things that most regularly comes through. As I have hinted, a lot of this is about power and the loss of power, and this is quite a double-edged matter. Some people have said, with some force, that we should be very careful here. We must think of people who are *silenced*, that is, people who lose their power because somebody else shuts them up. In Sara Maitland's wonderful *Book of Silence*, there's a letter that she prints from a friend of hers, Janet Batsleer, who argues, in effect that silence always means that someone is *being silenced*, so that it is 'the word' that is the beginning of freedom.[3] Janet talks at length and very passionately about the fact that silence can be a corrupting thing: 'Silence like a cancer, grows', as you'll remember from the great Simon and Garfunkel song of the 1960s, 'The Sound of Silence'.

But I think this is a wrong turn in the argument, even if for the right reasons. I hope I understand what's being said here – that when people's voices are silenced this is a very serious thing. It is of course supremely an exercise of power; to say I don't want to hear from you, I am telling you what counts here. But that's rather different from the silence that comes in the sort of context that I started with, the silence that comes when nobody is *trying* to silence you or rob you of your voice, but where somehow in the entire situation there is something else pressing in, which leaves you with nothing to say, the experience of helplessness about who you are, the experience of death and suffering, the experience of extraordinary depth and beauty. If we're silent in the face of these things it's not because we have been *shut* up; indeed you might say it's quite the opposite, it's because we've been *opened* up. And the silence that emerges there is not the silence of mute resentment, somebody else's oppression taking away my voice; it's a recognition of something that all human beings, powerful and powerless, sooner or later share, being up against what can't be mastered and managed. It's not *my* speech and *your* silence, it's *everybody's* silence in the face of these deep and difficult aspects of being human – and of course ultimately everybody's silence in the face of the utterly unmanageable, which is God.

The silence of the Christ

I am now going to turn to a couple of the ways in which the New Testament depicts significant silence. One of the most dramatic of these moments is Jesus' silence before his judges, before the High Priest and the Governor. The gospel narratives show us how the High Priest or Pontius Pilate urge Jesus to speak: 'Why don't you answer me?' says Pilate, 'Don't you know that I have the power to crucify you or to release you?' And we're told in St John's Gospel that when Jesus gives no answer to the charges made against him, Pilate wonders, he is 'amazed'. Now the odd thing in these stories is that Jesus is precisely in the position of someone having his voice taken away; he is a person who has been reduced to silence by the violence and injustice of the world he is in. But then, mysteriously, he turns this around. His silence, his complete presence and openness, his refusal to impose his will in a struggle, becomes a threat to those who have power – or think they have power. 'For God's sake, talk to me!' says the High Priest, more or less ('I adjure you in the name of the living God, tell us!'). And Pilate's wonderment, bafflement and fear in the face of Jesus' silence are a reminder that, in this case, Jesus as it were takes the powerlessness that has been forced on him and turns it around so that his silence becomes a place in the world where the mystery of God is present. In a small way, that's what happens when we seek to be truly and fully silent or let ourselves be silenced by the mystery of God. We become a 'place' where the mystery of God happens.

The sight of somebody praying or meditating in silence is itself something that reduces us to silence. If you go into a Buddhist meditation hall or a convent chapel and you see somebody deep in meditation, you don't on the whole, if you've got any sense, try to start a conversation – because the very fact that silence is happening tells us that there is something there that we're not going to cope with, something out of our normal repertoire of resources. And so Jesus' supreme, eloquent silence before his judges is, in a sense, the moment of supreme revelation in the Gospels. It is where he becomes visibly the mysterious reality that nobody knows how to talk about. 'Are you the Messiah, the Son of the Blessed One?' asks the High Priest, and Jesus says, 'If you want.' 'Are you the king of the Jews?' asks Pilate, and Jesus says, 'As you say.' And this terrible refusal to answer the question tells both Caiaphas and Pilate that what is happening in Jesus is something immeasurably out of the ordinary categories and habits by which people organize the world. That's why the strange thing about those stories is that they become themselves a moment of revelation, a moment of epiphany.

In all our theology and all our reflection on the person of Jesus, all the enormously complex and careful and sophisticated ways of talking we've evolved over the centuries about Jesus (rightly and inevitably), it's essential that we should let them lead us back to that moment of Jesus before his judges, that moment when *nobody knew what to call him*, because there were no words for God made human. What faced Caiaphas and Pilate was something so much out of any imaginable intellectual world that there was nothing to be said.

Let's pause for just a moment to consider this question of how we in our attempts to be silent become 'silencing' realities – the nun in the convent chapel or the meditator in the meditation hall who bring us to silence. We have to be to some extent, in our small way, like Jesus before the judges; we have to be the place where the question of God, the mystery of God, comes alive. It's not that we're saying and doing such devastatingly interesting things that we're blazing with holiness and mysteriousness in our ordinary lives (it would be very nice but it doesn't happen a lot). Rather, we will transmit something just by letting God be in us and showing as best we can that we're struggling to let God be, by holding back, recognizing that we are powerless to express, let alone to 'manage', the mystery.

I was struck recently while reading Julian of Norwich again by how much at the very heart of her vision there is the sense that all you've got to do in prayer is let God be God, remembering that Christ says to her, 'I am the ground of thy beseeching', I am your prayer.[4] That is the mystery that's going on when we try to pause, stop, be still, be in silence, let God occur. So often we try to convey or communicate the character and work of God to others by stepping up the noise and the activity; and yet for God to communicate who and what God is, God needs our silence.

> For God to communicate who and what God is, God needs our silence

Silence in worship

We can apply that to the liturgy of the Church. Good liturgy is about silence; I don't mean that good liturgy is all Quaker meeting (though one could do worse; and we often do) but that there's something about liturgy that ought to be pressing us in that direction. Here's something from the Anglican contemplative writer Maggie Ross:

> It is not a question of silence *or* speech, but rather that the transfiguring energy given in silence is expanded and integrated by making us attempt interpretation through speech, while in the same moment insights that arise from speech deepen and expand us again into the silence.[5]

She applies this to the language of worship: is the language we use in our worship something that flowers *out of* silence and patience and attention, and is this language something that leads us steadily back *into* silence and attention?

In quite a lot of the Church's history, both Catholic and Protestant traditions have variously got this wrong. There's been an urge to fill up the void, an anxiety about silence – whether it's the urge to improve the occasion and go on teaching, making sure that people are getting the right ideas, or the urge to keep things happening with lots of ceremonial. Both often seem rather to miss the point; busy and cluttered talk, like busy and cluttered activity, just tells people around that we're busy and that we're really rather anxious that they shouldn't get things wrong. Making space, acting, moving, speaking in a way that makes space around it, that's what liturgy needs to be. I think that is why people so often appreciate so deeply the liturgies of monastic communities, where space around the words happens quite naturally. People have the sense that the words are coming *out of* a steady, patient, attentiveness and they're going back *into* it; to listen to a monastic choir singing Compline is to listen to the opposite of busyness and to witness the opposite of fuss. We can't all be monastic choirs singing Compline, not every parish can be that. And yet it does seem to me a good question to be asking in the routine life of worship and liturgy in the Church: is our worship, are our words, the kind of thing that suggests moving out of and into that silence? Is the assembly gathered for the liturgy at least a little like the solitary nun in the convent chapel, something that silences people? So that the reaction of somebody who's not a believer coming into a worshipping community might in those circumstances not be 'That's interesting', but, 'I don't know what to make of this.' And that moment of 'I don't know what to make of this' becomes a really significant moment, something out of the ordinary controllable, manageable world, and begins to suggest the agency of reality pressing us in, drawing us forward.

In the last few decades, when we've been trying to reconstruct and rethink worship in the Anglican Church and the Roman Catholic Church and lots of others too, we've regularly made two sorts of mistake. We have said, 'It's all rather difficult, so we need to explain it'; and we have said, 'It's all rather long and we need to trim it.' The result is that we've lost sight of the ways in which the slow pace and the carefully chosen word, however mysterious, have their own integrity and their own effect. The result of this is that I am one of those people who don't know whether they're liturgical conservatives or liturgical progressives. I lose no sleep over this: because when we think about liturgy and shared worship, what we have *most* to think about is whether the actions and the words performed convey any sense that something is happening that nobody *there* is doing – if you see what I mean. And liturgy comes alive when that's the sense people have, whatever form the liturgy is taking.

I was preaching a sermon a little while ago to the Guild of Church Organists, talking to them about the experience that many organists have of something like awe at the *scale* of the instrument. You put one finger on a small ivory button and something shattering is released. The organist using his or her skills and muscles and intelligence produces an effect massively out of proportion to what this fragile human presence on the bench is apparently doing. And that is very much an aspect of how good liturgy works. I began that sermon by quoting *Winnie the Pooh* (which is a great temptation on many occasions): you may remember when a storm blows over Owl's house and wrecks all his furniture, and the tree is lying on the ground; Pooh picks himself up from the ground afterwards and asks, 'Did I do that?'[6] Coming out of liturgy and saying, 'Did I do that?' is a perfectly proper experience. Something happens that nobody in particular has done. Of course I didn't, and no one did; but something was released.

So whether we're talking about the individual impact of the praying, meditating, contemplating person or the *corporate* impact of a community that has found itself in that kind of environment and framework, the same thing applies. We're back to where we started, in that territory where we can't get on top of something – we can't domesticate, organize, control. This is a necessary aspect of being human, it is a necessary aspect of faith and, if my reading of the Gospels is right, it is a necessary dimension of our following of Christ, part of what the Holy Spirit makes possible in us as we are made more Christ-like.

Silence before God

When we think about how we are to be silent before God, we're faced with the ultimate paradox. How do you try to stop trying? And of course the only way of doing it is not to try. That is why the way we use words and physical practices to settle ourselves becomes very important in living our way into deeper silence. We want to 'give God a chance' to happen where we are. How do we do it? Well, we could sit down and say, 'I'm going to be silent, I'm really going to concentrate on God'; we all know how completely useless that is. Or we can sit down and say, 'Lord Jesus Christ, Son of God, have mercy on me a sinner', or, 'My Lord and my God', or, 'Jesu, lover of my soul', saying those words until they're rubbed so smooth you barely notice they're there. You can watch your breath, you can be conscious of your diaphragm rising and falling, conscious of the movement of life in you, and if you *think* at all about it you might just think, 'Well, for this time as

I breathe in and out, all I am is a place where life is happening.' The breath moves in, the breath moves out; I am a place where life is happening. And if I am a place where life is happening, I am a place where *God* is happening. So the physical settling, the words we choose to take us into silence, these things matter very deeply because they're part of the raw materials of taking us gently but firmly out of our depth – which is where we belong. They're part of that letting go of power and anxiety that is such a central and essential part of becoming a disciple.

It helps sometimes to think of all the ordinary prosaic experiences of being brought to silence that we started with, lest anybody should suppose that Christian contemplation, or any other kind of contemplation, is something eccentric and unnatural. The fact is that for us to be human at all we need those moments, those extraordinary moments of being pushed out of our depth. It's human; don't panic! And the silence that expresses and embodies and educates

> *For us to be human at all we need those moments, those extraordinary moments of being pushed out of our depth*

in faith is not something completely different in kind, which is why it doesn't do any harm to be aware in our ordinary lives of those moments when we're at a loss. If we're someone who keeps a spiritual journal, it doesn't hurt to register the times when that's how we experience something; the moment in a conversation, the moment in a walk in the street or a journey in the tube, the moment when we're watching television, the moment at the end of the play or the concert, those moments when we don't know what to say, and recognize that that's the most important thing that's happened.

In thinking about this, it helps also to make the connection with that extraordinary upside-down moment in the Gospels when the helpless Jesus who has been silenced mysteriously makes his silence and his powerlessness a way of presence and speech, and indeed judgement. We pray with all humility that when we try to be seriously silent in this way, something of what Caiaphas and Pilate saw just might be visible in us – so long of course as we never *think* of it; that's another of the great catches of silence. As St Anthony of Egypt says, 'If you know that you're praying, you're really not.' Nonetheless, it isn't a mark of damaging pride or self-consciousness to have those simple handrails, those words and physical discip-lines that give us something to think about other than just 'silence'. We're not thinking about being silent, we're using words, using the breath, using our posture just to be there.

God is God by being God for us, and we are human by being human for God

We're letting God be God, and in the process we're letting ourselves become more fully human, because, in the extraordinary economy of heaven, God is God by being God for us, and we are human by being human for God; and all joy and fulfilment opens up once we recognize this.

For reflection or discussion

1 What is your attitude to silence? What are the positive and humanly constructive ways in which you might use it?

2 Why do you think some people find that practising forms of silent or contemplative prayer helps them to draw closer to God?

Epilogue: Humanity transfigured

The Feast of the Ascension is one of the most significant days in the Church's liturgical calendar. It celebrates Christ's return to the Father 40 days after his resurrection (Acts 1.1–11). 'I came from the Father', says Jesus in John's Gospel, 'and have come into the world; again, I am leaving the world and am going to the Father' (John 16.28).

One popular hymn for the Feast of the Ascension contains these lines:

> Thou hast raised our human nature
> In the clouds to God's right hand.[1]

The Ascension of Jesus in this context becomes a celebration of the extraordinary fact that our humanity in all its variety and its vulnerability has been taken by Jesus into the heart of the divine life. 'Man with God is on the throne', the hymn goes on: quite a shocking line if you start thinking about it.

It is, first of all, good news about humanity itself – the humanity that we all know to be stained, wounded, imprisoned in various ways. This humanity – yours and mine – is still capable of being embraced by God, shot through with God's glory, received and welcomed in the burning heart of reality itself. As another hymn puts it, we are welcomed

106

To the throne of Godhead,
To the Father's breast.[2]

Let's pursue that theme just a little bit further. Jesus takes our human nature – yours and mine – to the heart of

God, and he speaks to God his Father in a human voice. In heaven, the language they speak is human, not just angelic. Our words, human words, are heard at the very centre of that burning heart of reality.

> *Jesus takes our human nature – yours and mine – to the heart of God*

St Augustine reflected on this in his many sermons on the psalms. Like most of us, he was rather worried by the fact that the psalms are not always fit for polite company. They are full of rude, angry, violent, hateful remarks; they contain protests against God and spectacular ill-wishing against human beings. The psalms, you might say, are as human as it gets. So why do we recite them in public worship? Aren't they just a reminder of those aspects of our humanity that are best left out of God's sight?

Augustine's point was this: apart from the fact that it is no use trying to leave bits of our humanity out of God's sight, God has actually taken an *initiative* in making our language his own. And therefore you have to imagine, as you say or hear the psalms, that Jesus is speaking them. And there's another shocking thought – *Jesus* saying, 'Where

are you, God?' *Jesus* saying, 'My God, why have you for-
saken me?' (But then of course he did.) *Jesus* saying, 'Destroy
my enemies' and 'Blessed are those who dash their children
against the stones' . . . goodness knows what. Well, says the
saint, it doesn't mean that Jesus is telling us that any and
every human cry is good. It doesn't mean that Jesus endor-
ses ideas about revenge on our enemies, or even shaking
our fists at God the Father. But it does mean that Jesus
treats us, our feelings, our tumultuous personalities, as *real*.
He takes us seriously. He takes us seriously when we're
moving towards God and each other in love; and, amaz-
ingly, he takes us seriously when we're moving in the opposite direction – when we are spinning downwards into
destructive, hateful fantasies. He doesn't let go of us and
he doesn't lose sight of us when we seek to lock ourselves
up in the dark. Jesus hears all the words we speak – words
of pain and protest and rage and violence. He hears them
and he takes them, and in the presence of God the Father
he says, 'This is the humanity I have brought home. It's
not a pretty sight; it's not edifying and impressive and
heroic, it's just real: real and needy and confused, and here
it is (this complicated humanity) brought home to heaven,
dropped into the burning heart of God – for healing and
for transformation.' That's quite a lot to bear in mind when
you're saying or hearing the psalms. But it's probably the
only way of coping with rather a lot of them.

But all of that in the saint's thinking arises from this basic insight: Jesus ascends to heaven. The human life in which God has made himself most visible, most tangible, disappears from the human world in its former shape and is somehow absorbed into the endless life of God. And our humanity, all of it, goes with Jesus. When St Paul speaks of Christ 'filling all in all' (Ephesians 1.15–end), we must bear in mind that picture: Jesus' humanity taking into it all the difficult, resistant, unpleasant bits of our humanity, taking them into the heart of love where alone they can be healed and transfigured. And when in Acts (1.1–11) Jesus speaks of the Holy Spirit as the 'promise of the Father' that is going to descend on the world, he's speaking of the way in which the gift of the Holy Spirit of God enables us not only to *be* a new kind of being but to *see* human beings afresh and to hear them differently. When the Holy Spirit sweeps over us in the wind and the flame of Pentecost, the Holy Spirit gives us the life of Jesus. It gives us something of Jesus' capacity to hear what is really being said by human beings. It gives us the courage not to screen out those bits of the human world that are difficult, unpleasant, those that are not edifying. It opens our eyes and our ears and our hearts to the full range of what being human means. So that, instead

> *The Holy Spirit opens our eyes and our ears and our hearts to the full range of what being human means*

of being somebody who needs to be sheltered from the rough truth of the world, the Christian is someone who should be *more* open and *more* vulnerable to that great range of human experience. The Christian is not in a position to censor out any bits of the human voice, that troubling symphony which so often draws into itself pain, anger and violence. And to recognize that we're open to that and we hear it is not about shrugging our shoulders and saying, 'Well, that's just human nature' (one of the most unhelpful phrases in the moral vocabulary). On the contrary, we feel the edge, the ache in human anger and human suffering. And we recognize that it can be taken *into* Christ and *into* the heart of the Father. It can be healed. It can be transfigured.

Jesus has gone before us into the darkest places of human reality. He has picked up the sounds that he hears. And think of what those sounds are: the quiet cries of the abused child; the despairing tears of a refugee, of a woman in the Middle East, surrounded and threatened by different kinds of mindless violence; the fear of a man watching a flood or hurricane destroying his family's livelihood. Jesus picks up the cry of the hungry and the forgotten. He hears the human beings that nobody else hears. And he calls to us to say, '*You* listen too.' He makes his own the cynical dismissal of faith by the sophisticated, and sees through it to the underlying need. He makes his own the joy and celebration and thanksgiving of human beings going about their routine work and finding their fulfilment in ordinary, prosaic, everyday love and faithfulness. All of that is taken 'To the throne of Godhead, / To the Father's breast', to the burning heart of truth and reality.

Notes

1 What is consciousness?

1 Stanislas Dehaene, *Consciousness and the Brain: Deciphering How the Brain Codes Our Thoughts* (New York, Viking Press, 2014).

2 Edith Stein, *On the Problem of Empathy* (Washington, DC, Institute of Carmelite Studies, 2nd edn, 1989).

3 Iain McGilchrist, *The Master and His Emissary* (New Haven, CT, Yale University Press, 2009).

4 Raymond Tallis, *Reflections of a Metaphysical Flâneur* (Abingdon and New York, Routledge, 2014).

5 Quoted in Tallis, *Reflections of a Metaphysical Flâneur*, p. 164.

6 Daniel Dennett, *Consciousness Explained* (Boston, MA, Little Brown, 1991).

7 Ludwig Wittgenstein, *Lectures and Conversations on Aesthetics, Psychology and Religious Belief* (Oxford, Blackwell, 1966), pp. 23–4.

8 John Gray, *The Soul of the Marionette: A Short Enquiry into Human Freedom* (London: Allen Lane, 2015).

2 What is a person?

1 Vladimir Lossky, 'The Theological Notion of the Human Person' in *In the Image and Likeness of God* (New York, St Vladimir's Seminary Press, 1974), p. 120.

2 Robert Spaemann, *Essays in Anthropology* (Eugene, OR, Cascade Books, 2010), p. 19.

3 Richard Sennett, *Together: The Rituals, Pleasures and Politics of Co-operation* (London, Allen Lane, 2012), p. 115.

4 Sennett, *Together*, p. 188, quoting Alexis de Tocqueville, *Democracy in America*, trans. and ed. H. C. Mansfield and D. Winthrop (Chicago, IL, University of Chicago Press, 2002).

5 Patricia Gosling, *Fatal Flaws* (London, Lulu, 2012), p. 12.

6 Sennett, *Together*, p. 219.

3 Bodies, minds and thoughts

1 Iain McGilchrist, *The Master and His Emissary* (New Haven, CT, Yale University Press, 2009).

2 Shepherd is a philosopher who has written extensively about the ways in which the body itself 'thinks' by way of the various focal points of the nervous system.

3 Richard Sennett, *The Craftsman* (New Haven, CT, Yale University Press, 2008).

4 Jo Guldi and David Armitage, *The History Manifesto* (Cambridge, Cambridge University Press, 2014).

5 Edith Stein, *On the Problem of Empathy* (Washington, DC, Institute of Carmelite Studies, 2nd edn, 1989).

6 Augustine, *Confessions* VII.17–18.

4 Faith and human flourishing

1 Søren Kierkegaard, quoted in Ernest Becker, *The Denial of Death* (New York, The Free Press, 1997), p. 84.

2 Ernest Becker, *The Denial of Death* (New York, The Free Press, 1997), e.g. pp. 84–5.

3 Thomas Ken, 'Awake my soul' (1674).

4 Richard Sennett, *The Corrosion of Character: The Personal Consequences of Work in the New Capitalism* (New York, W. W. Norton & Co., 1998).

5 Silence and human maturity

1 Richard Hooker, *Of the Laws of Ecclesiastical Polity* 1.2.

2 John of the Cross, *Spiritual Canticle* 9.4.

3 Sara Maitland, *A Book of Silence* (London, Granta, 2008), p. 28.

4 Julian of Norwich, *Revelations of Divine Love*, ch. 41.

5 Maggie Ross, *Writing the Icon of the Heart: In Silence Beholding* (Eugene, OR, Cascade Books, 2013), p. 89.

6 A. A. Milne, *The House at Pooh Corner* (London, Methuen & Co., 1928), ch. 8.

Epilogue: Humanity transfigured

1 Christopher Wordsworth, 'See the Conqueror mounts in triumph' (1862).
2 Caroline M. Noel, 'At the name of Jesus' (1870).

Further reading

Ernest Becker, *The Denial of Death* (New York, The Free Press, 1997).

Stanislas Dehaene, *Consciousness and the Brain: Deciphering How the Brain Codes Our Thoughts* (New York, Viking Press, 2014).

Daniel Dennett, *Consciousness Explained* (Boston, MA, Little Brown, 1991).

Patricia Gosling, *Fatal Flaws* (London, Lulu, 2012).

John Gray, *The Soul of the Marionette: A Short Enquiry into Human Freedom* (London: Allen Lane, 2015).

Jo Guldi and David Armitage, *The History Manifesto* (Cambridge, Cambridge University Press, 2014).

John of the Cross, *Spiritual Canticle.*

Julian of Norwich, *Revelations of Divine Love.*

Vladimir Lossky, 'The Theological Notion of the Human Person' in *In the Image and Likeness of God* (New York, St Vladimir's Seminary Press, 1974).

Iain McGilchrist, *The Master and His Emissary* (New Haven, CT, Yale University Press, 2009).

Sara Maitland, *A Book of Silence* (London, Granta, 2008).

Maggie Ross, *Writing the Icon of the Heart: In Silence Beholding* (Eugene, OR, Cascade Books, 2013).

Richard Sennett, *The Corrosion of Character: The Personal Consequences of Work in the New Capitalism* (New York, W. W. Norton & Co., 1998).

Richard Sennett, *The Craftsman* (New Haven, CT, Yale University Press, 2008).

Richard Sennett, *Together: The Rituals, Pleasures and Politics of Co-operation* (London, Allen Lane, 2012).

Philip Shepherd, *New Self, New World: Recovering Our Senses in the Twenty-first Century* (Berkeley, CA, North Atlantic Books, 2010).

Robert Spaemann, *Essays in Anthropology* (Eugene, OR, Cascade Books, 2010).

Further reading

Raymond Tallis, *Reflections of a Metaphysical Flâneur* (Abingdon and New York, Routledge, 2014).

Ludwig Wittgenstein, *Lectures and Conversations on Aesthetics, Psychology and Religious Belief* (Oxford, Blackwell, 1966).

Acknowledgements

The chapters in this book are based on addresses originally given between 2009 and 2015, as follows:

Chapter 1   **What is consciousness?**
             James Gregory Lecture, University of St Andrews, 13 April 2015.

Chapter 2   **The person and the individual: human dignity, human relationships and human limits**
             Fifth Annual Theos Lecture, London, 1 October 2012.

Chapter 3   **The tree of knowledge: bodies, minds and thoughts**
             Lecture at Durham Castle, 18 February 2015.

Chapter 4   **Faith and human flourishing: religious belief and ideals of maturity**
             Lecture as Humanitas Visiting Professor in Interfaith Studies, University of Oxford, 29 January 2014.

Chapter 5   **What grows in the gaps: silence and human maturing**
             Talk in the Silence in the City series, Westminster Cathedral Hall, 4 May 2014.

Epilogue   **A sermon at the Ascension Day Sung Eucharist**
             Westminster Abbey, 21 May 2009.